Library of
Davidson College

Library of
Davidson College

THE PRESENCE OF STOICISM
IN MEDIEVAL THOUGHT

THE PRESENCE OF STOICISM IN MEDIEVAL THOUGHT

by

Gerard Verbeke

The Catholic University of America Press
Washington, D.C.

Copyright © 1983
The Catholic University of America Press
All rights reserved
Printed in the United States of America

Library of Congress Cataloging in Publication Data

Verbeke, Gerard.
　The presence of Stoicism in medieval thought.

　Includes indexes.
　　1. Stoics—History—Addresses, essays, lectures.
　　2. Philosophy, Medieval—Addresses, essays, lectures.
　　I. Title.
B528.V4　　　188　　　　　　　82-4134
ISBN 0-8132-0572-7 (cl)　　　　　AACR2
ISBN 0-8132-0573-5 (pa)

CONTENTS

Preface vii
Chapter I: Medieval Acquaintance with Stoicism 1
Chapter II: The Challenge of Materialism 21
Chapter III: Ethical Perspectives 45
Chapter IV: Fatalism and Freedom 71
Index of Names 97
Index of Topics 101

PREFACE

When Martin Grabmann was an old man, he once stated that it is easier to write big books than it is to die. This may be true, and yet in some cases it is very difficult to compose a respectable book about a particular topic in medieval thought. When a subject is fairly circumscribed, when it falls within clearly defined limits, it may be easy to treat of it and its various aspects without running the risk of serious mistakes or unforgivable omissions. If, however, an issue is very broad and touches on many authors over a long period of time, then it will be very difficult to grasp it in its many facets. This happens to be true of the present task. The Middle Ages cover a period of ten centuries and include many important authors and writings which in one way or another manifest the presence of Stoic ideas and doctrines. The main difficulty in studying the topic under consideration is the fact that in many instances medieval authors themselves were unaware of their having anything to do with Stoicism. This philosophy had been gradually assimilated even from the first centuries of the Christian era, so that its legacy was passed on to later generations without being identified as Stoic. Moreover, when assimilated and rethought by Christian writers, Stoic doctrines did not always remain the same. They were transformed and adapted as they were incorporated into a new context. The notions of natural law and fate are typical illustrations of this progressive transformation under the influence of a new intellectual climate. Hence one can readily understand why medieval thinkers did not always recognize their indebtedness to Stoic ideas and doctrines.

Beginning from a careful study of the Stoic fragments and writings which have survived, I have attempted to uncover the frequently hidden life of philosophical notions and doctrines through the course of history. If a heritage from the past is transmitted in its authentic and original form, it can easily be recognized. But Stoic philosophy was always a living thought. Being a philosophy of life, it was in itself a piece of life. With all of these difficulties in mind, I hesitated to write this small book. When I finally decided to attempt it, I wished to draft only an introduction to the topic, a kind of first approach that might serve as a stimulus for further research. Here I do not deal with the Stoic theory of knowledge or with Stoic logic

PREFACE

(including philosophy of language), although I assume that these doctrines also influenced later thought. These issues could better be treated in a separate study after they have been more thoroughly investigated in medieval writings. Nor do I examine fully certain other elements of Stoic philosophy, for instance its important teaching on seminal reasons and the organic evolution of the world.

In dealing with the presence of Stoicism in medieval thought, my first concern was to find an appropriate method. I immediately realized that it would be tedious to treat all medieval authors in chronological sequence and to examine each for the degree to which he was influenced by Stoic ideas. Therefore I have chosen a thematic approach by singling out certain basic aspects of Stoic thought in order to determine whether and to what extent they have survived in medieval philosophy. The choice of the issues to be treated was rather obvious. Having provisionally set aside the whole area of dialectics, I had to face problems from physics and ethics. In these fields it was necessary for me to treat the questions of materialism, necessity and freedom, and natural law, together with the connected notions of synderesis and conscience. The first chapter was indispensable in order for me to show how Stoicism penetrated into the Middle Ages.

The immediate occasion giving rise to this essay was a series of lectures I was invited to deliver at The Catholic University of America in Washington, D.C., in March, 1981. I am deeply grateful to Professor Jude P. Dougherty, Dean of the School of Philosophy, who kindly invited me to give these lectures and who suggested the topic I actually treated. It was an honor and a pleasure for me to accept this invitation, and I am proud to have had the opportunity to lecture at this excellent School of Philosophy. I am grateful also to John F. Wippel, a former Louvain student and now a professor at The Catholic University, for having read my text and introduced some stylistic changes in preparation for its publication.

Brussels, August 1, 1981

CHAPTER I

MEDIEVAL ACQUAINTANCE WITH STOICISM

Some years ago a famous medievalist stated that the medieval period was a "nice" time, since Stoicism was ignored.[1] One can hardly agree with this. Whether or not the medieval period was a "nice" time is an open question. From the Renaissance onward widely divergent evaluations of medieval civilization have been proposed.[2] Whatever its value may be, the medieval period did not ignore Stoicism. Stoic philosophy was present in the intellectual life of that time and played an important role in the evolution of medieval thought, especially so until the time of the overpowering introduction of Aristotelian writings. But even then some Stoic doctrines, primarily in the field of ethics, continued to be a force in shaping medieval philosophy and theology. And yet the abovementioned statement is not entirely mistaken. At no particular time during the Middle Ages was there an invasion of Stoicism. There was never a massive introduction of Stoic philosophical writings into the Latin West by means of translations. The assimilation of Stoic ideas and doctrines at that time was largely unconscious, since it had already commenced before the beginning of the medieval era.

* * *

For five centuries, that is to say, during the entire Hellenistic

---

[1]Cf. M. Spanneut, *Permanence du Stoïcisme de Zénon à Malraux* (Gembloux, 1973), p. 209: "Le Moyen Age était le beau temps. Il ignorait le Stoïcisme."

[2]In her fascinating book entitled *Pour en finir avec le moyen âge* (Paris, 1977), Régine Pernoud, dealing with the meaning of the term "Renaissance," quotes a passage from the *Dictionnaire général des lettres*, published in 1872: "Les Arts et les Lettres, qui paraissaient avoir péri dans le même naufrage que la société romaine, semblèrent refleurir et après dix siècles de ténèbres, briller d'un nouvel éclat."

period, Stoicism was the predominant philosophy. At that time the influence exercised by other philosophical schools was not strong.[3] Epicureanism came into being when Zeno of Citium, the founder of the Stoic School, began to teach at Athens. Epicurus and his followers never took part in public life. Instead they formed a small community of friends and lived apart from the troubles of political and social life in order to protect their peace of mind.[4] As to the Peripatetic School, it continued on, but without always remaining faithful to Aristotelian teaching. In the middle of the first century B.C., a full edition of Aristotle's works was completed and more and more commentaries were devoted to his writings.[5] The School of Plato also continued to be active, but without adhering to any coherent and comprehensive philosophical system. Representatives of this school rather opposed and criticized the teaching of "dogmatic" philosophers instead of maintaining a theory of their own.[6] This is even truer of the skeptical movements of that time. Because they maintained the impossibility of attaining certainty, they could hardly present a coherent interpretation of man and the world. Finally, the Pythagorean movement also still existed during the Hellenistic period, but without penetrating into the masses. That would have been quite contrary to the spirit of its founder, who rather wanted to establish some aristocratic groups which would

---

[3]Cf. G. Verbeke, "Le Stoïcisme, une philosophie sans frontières," in *Aufstieg und Niedergang der römischen Welt*, I: *Von den Anfängen Roms bis zum Ausgang der Republik*, 4. Band (Berlin-New York, 1973), pp. 3–42.

[4]The ideal of "ataraxia," tranquillity of mind, totally dominates Epicurean thinking. The term "ataraxia" has a negative meaning, it refers to the absence of something, i.e., the absence of whatever jeopardizes internal freedom and peace: "Il fallait donc chercher en soi-même une liberté intérieure qui affranchit des hommes: la vie *adespotos*, 'sans maître', voilà l'un des mots typiques de la nouvelle sagesse (Epicure, *Ep.*, III, 133; encore Sallustius, 21)" (A.J. Festugière, *Epicure et ses dieux* [Paris, 1946], p. ix).

[5]Owing to the edition of Andronicos of Rhodos, a genuine renaissance of Aristotle began: "Mit Andronikos stehen wir an einem entscheidenden Wendepunkt in der Geschichte des Aristotelismus, denn er war es, der durch seine Edition der Nachwelt den Zugang zu Aristoteles öffnete" (I. Düring, *Aristoteles, Darstellung und Interpretation seines Denkens* [Heidelberg, 1966], p. 39).

[6]According to G. Reale, Arcesilaos was clearly influenced by Pyrrhonian skepticism: this skeptical trend was fused with similar elements taken from Socrates and Plato (*Storia della filosofia antica*, vol. III, *I sistemi dell'età ellenistica* [Milan, 1976], p. 501).

embody in practice Pythagoras's ideal of religious and moral life.⁷ At that time Stoicism was the only philosophy which addressed its message to all human beings without distinction and which extended its influence throughout the then known world.

How is one to account for this persistent and widespread influence of Stoicism? It must be related to certain characteristic features of its philosophy which apparently answered to the needs and aspirations of large groups of people. Stoicism was from its very beginning a doctrine of internal liberation. According to its teaching, almost all men live in a permanent condition of slavery since they are subjected to their passions and emotions. Instead of living in accord with reason, which itself is a particle of the immanent divine Spirit, they are dominated within themselves by every kind of irrational movement. The main objective of these philosophers was to free man from those impulses which constantly push him to pursue goals which, being indifferent, are without any real value. The remarkable privilege of the Stoic sage is to be free and self-sufficient, even under life's heaviest burdens.

The Stoics' teaching on internal liberation is quite in agreement with their new interpretation of traditional fatalism. The entire evolution of the cosmos is determined by an immanent rational principle that regulates whatever occurs in the world. Owing to this new interpretation, the traditional concept of fatalism was thoroughly transformed.⁸

A final factor that explains Stoicism's influence is its teaching that all human beings—free citizens and slaves, men and women, Greeks and barbarians—are fundamentally equal. Traditionally it had been

---

⁷One of the characteristic features of the Neo-Pythagorean School is its mystical tendency. Its philosophical message is more than the result of human research. It is thought to be a divine revelation. Pythagoras is not merely a philosopher. He is regarded as a prophet (G. Reale, *Storia della filosofia antica*, vol. IV, *Le scuole dell'età imperiale* [Milan, 1978], p. 390).

⁸In his famous *Hymn to Zeus* Cleanthes does not ask God to change the course of events. He could hardly do this, since the whole history of the cosmos is regulated from within by divine Reason. A wise man never opposes the development of events. This evolution can only be rational since it stems from the divine principle. Cleanthes asks God to take away the darkness from his soul, so that he may see and recognize the divine law that governs the world (*Stoicorum Veterum Fragmenta*, vol. I, fr. 537, 29–30).

held that free citizens were naturally superior to slaves, men to women, and Greeks to barbarians. Even Aristotle admits that some individuals are slaves by nature, and that women and barbarians represent a lower level of humanity. Quite in agreement with their own physical system, the Stoics reject such discrimination. The soul of each human individual, whatever his rank in society, is a particle of the divine Spirit.[9] According to Seneca, no one can be completely reduced to slavery.[10] Without being put into practice immediately, this doctrine deeply influenced the subsequent development of civilization.[11]

What about the later period, one may ask. Did Stoicism's influence cease during the third century, when Neoplatonism became the dominant philosophical current? No, it did not, and in part because Neoplatonism itself was not free from Stoic influences. In many ways, it is true, there is opposition between these two philosophical systems. Neoplatonism is a highly spiritualistic interpretation of reality, according to which everything flows from the three principal hypostases. Stoicism is a kind of materialistic pantheism, and teaches that even the immanent divine Spirit is corporeal. On the other hand, there are also striking affinities. The doctrine of seminal reasons plays an important part in both philosophies. Originally, however, it belonged to Stoicism. Aristotle had explained becoming and movement by means of potency and act. The Stoics interpret each movement as the evolving of hidden possibilities, the growth of seeds in which all the elements of any later development are already contained.[12] In Plotinus's thought, seminal reasons are a

---

[9]G. Verbeke, "Le Stoïcisme, une philosophie sans frontières," pp. 4–5.

[10]Seneca, *De ben.*, III, 20: Errat, si quis existimat servitutem in totum hominem descendere: pars melior eius excepta est. . . . Corpus itaque est, quod domino fortuna tradidit. Hoc emit, hoc vendit: interior ea pars mancipio dari non potest.

[11]The Stoics did not demand the abolition of slavery as a social institution. Was this a lack of logical coherence and practical consistency on their part? Not really. We should not forget that in their view man's social condition is something indifferent (ἀδιάφορον). What matters is moral virtue. This moral perfection is also attainable by slaves and women.

[12]According to Zeno, the divine principle is the seminal reason of the cosmos. This means that the variety of beings develops from an original seed that already contains within itself all the elements of the later evolution (Diog. Laërt., VII, 135, 136 [*SVF* I, 102]; G. Verbeke, "Les Stoïciens et le progrès de l'histoire," *Revue philosophique de Louvain* 62 [1964], p. 7).

link between the intelligible objects in the second hypostasis—Intelligence—and the created world. Seminal reasons immediately proceed from universal Soul and shape the world according to the intelligible pattern. In this respect as in others the affinity between the two systems is undeniable. Given this, it follows that Stoic doctrines also penetrated into the West through the channel of Neoplatonic writings.

It is also true, however, that Stoicism's influence on Western civilization began long before the birth of Neoplatonism. Its influence may already be noticed in Rome during the second century B.C. and is connected with names such as Panaetius and Posidonius. Therefore, it is not surprising that Stoicism exercised some influence on Christian authors at a very early point.[13] Christian moral teaching was influenced by Stoic categories at an early date. Among Greek Christian writers one may cite Clement of Alexandria, Origen, Gregory of Nyssa, and Nemesius of Emesa. Some of their works were eventually translated into Latin and could be read directly by Western philosophers and theologians. Some Latin Christian writers also passed on the Stoic legacy to later generations. Among these may be mentioned Tertullian, Lactantius, Saint Jerome, Saint Ambrose, and Saint Augustine.[14]

By the beginning of the Middle Ages a legacy of Stoic ideas had already been accepted and assimilated by Christian writers, Greek as well as Latin. At no particular moment of the Christian era did Stoicism suddenly burst upon the scene. It rather exercised its influence in a permanent way without provoking any major reaction or crisis. Stoicism was never condemned by the Church as incompatible with Christian orthodoxy. Aristotelianism had to face many difficulties and much opposition during the first centuries of Christianity. Christians were openly hostile to Aristotle. They took him to task for having denied divine providence, for having rejected immortality of the soul, and for having defended the eternity of the world. During the first half of the medieval period, one could study the logic of the Stagirite because of the Boethian translations and commentaries. It was only in the twelfth century that the Latin West

---

[13] G. Verbeke, "Le Stoïcisme, une philosophie sans frontières," pp. 35–40.
[14] M. Spanneut, *Le Stoïcisme des Pères de l'Eglise de Clément de Rome à Clément d'Alexandrie* (Paris, 1969); *Permanence du Stoïcisme de Zénon à Malraux*, pp. 138–78.

could gradually begin to read other treatises by the Greek Master. In the second half of the thirteenth century these new translations gave rise to the crisis of heterodox Aristotelianism.[15] One can describe with sufficient accuracy the various stages of Aristotelianism's penetration into the West, but this is not possible in the case of Stoicism. It is always present, but without being in the foreground.

Aristotle's works were gradually translated into Latin, some of them earlier than others. Some were translated more than once, or at least earlier versions were corrected and revised. These translations quickly spread and were carefully studied, especially in the newly founded Universities. Because of the recent publications of the *Aristoteles latinus*, we are now fairly well informed about the ups and downs involved in this translation activity and in Aristotelianism's progressive penetration into the West. For each period of the Middle Ages we know which treatises of Aristotle were available to the Latin reader. Here again the situation with Stoicism is quite different. During the course of the Middle Ages the number of available Stoic sources hardly increased at all. The writings of the main representatives of the Stoic School were not translated into Latin. Except for those of the later Stoics, they were not even available in the original Greek. Not a single writing from the earlier

---

[15]Platonism and Stoicism were never condemned by Church authorities. Were these philosophical systems more compatible with Christian belief than Aristotelianism? Actually no, but the integration of those doctrines proceeded gradually. From the beginning of the Christian era Platonic spiritualism and Stoic ethics were assimilated. These teachings were to some extent transformed and adapted to Christian belief, and so there never was a frontal clash between these philosophical systems and the Christian Church. The penetration of Aristotelianism into the West was different. The translation movement from Greek and Arabic started in the twelfth century. Already in the thirteenth century some philosophers and theologians in the West so strongly accepted Aristotle's thought that they believed this system to be irrefutable from a philosophical standpoint, even though they wanted to remain Christians. Consequently, they proclaimed a divergence between rational truth and Christian belief. They did not want to abandon their Christian belief although it was in disagreement with philosophical truth. This question is very basic and ultimately refers to the relationship between nature and grace, science and revelation. The intervention of the Church was intended to be a warning to the Christians, asking them not to accept as philosophical truth a doctrine that is incompatible with the Christian message.

Stoics has survived. We only have some fragments which are usually not literal quotations from the original works. Apart from some information provided by Greek and Arabic commentaries, a Latin reader of the thirteenth or fourteenth century was hardly better off than one at the beginning of the medieval period. The number of sources available to him had hardly increased. Even Epictetus's *Enchiridion* was not translated into Latin before the fifteenth century. Niccolo Pirotti's version was completed in July, 1450,[16] and that by Angelus Politian was first published at Bologna in 1497.[17] If the study of Aristotelianism's penetration into the West is closely connected with the spread of newly translated sources, this method cannot be applied to an examination of Stoic influences in the Middle Ages. Here we must determine whether the sources already available from the beginning of the Christian era were still being read and commented upon, or whether they were rather eclipsed by other works and intellectual trends.

In fact, Stoic ideas and doctrines penetrated into the Latin West through many channels. Some Greek commentaries on Aristotle were translated into Latin during the thirteenth century. Several of these provide important information about Stoic thought, especially Simplicius's Commentary on the *Categories*.[18] Some writings by Arab-speaking philosophers were also translated into Latin. According to Osman Amin, there was much sympathy for Stoic ethics among Arab philosophers.[19] Even classical literary authors passed on some ideas and teachings that originally stem from Stoic sources. The same is true of several early Christian writers.

To mention all the works through which Stoic information and Stoic ideas were introduced into the Middle Ages would be a gigantic task. Here we must limit ourselves to those that are most impor-

---

[16]Cf. *Niccolo Pirotti's Version of the Enchiridion of Epictetus*, edited with an introduction and a list of Pirotti's writings by Revilo Pendleton Oliver (Urbana, 1954), pp. 81–136.

[17]*Angeli Politiani in Epicteti Stoici Enchiridion, e graeco a se interpretatum ad Laurentium Mediceum Epistola*, edited by Philippus Beroaldus (Bologna, 1497); cf. L. Hain, *Repertorium bibliographicum*, I (Berlin, 1925), no. 4847.

[18]The Latin version of this important commentary has been edited by A. Pattin in the *Corpus latinum commentariorum in Aristotelem graecorum*.

[19]Osman Amin, "Stoic Ethics in Classical Arabic Culture," in *Actas del V. Congreso internacional de Filosofia Medieval* (Madrid), I, pp. 89–94.

tant. For a Latin reader in the West a first source of information about Stoicism was Seneca. His writings were available in medieval libraries. Many twelfth-century thinkers read and studied at least some of Seneca's works, though they confused him with the rhetor, his father.[20] Almost all of these writers are very much in favor of Seneca. They view him as an exceptional sage.[21] John of Salisbury writes of him: "He is a keen Stoic; he grasps the core of moral behavior and always expresses adequately what he has in mind" (*Stoicus est acer, morum compendia captat / Verbaque semper habet sensibus apta suis*).[22] This is quite different from Quintilian's judgment about Seneca.[23] The fact that the correspondence between Seneca and St. Paul was thought to be authentic contributed to the admiration for this philosopher. Philip of Harvengt's attitude is quite significant in this respect. He believes that Seneca pointed out to St. Paul how he should behave toward the Thessalonians.[24] According to John of Salisbury in the *Policraticus*, Seneca is always a faithful guardian of moral behavior and opposed to any kind of immorality.[25] Godfrey of St. Victor's judgment is equally favorable. He writes in his *Fons philosophiae* that Seneca addressed to Lucilius some recommendations that are comparable to the teaching of the Gospels.[26] Alan of Lille writes in his *Anticlaudianus* that Seneca, in following the guidance of reason, is a master of moral education.[27] In his *Dialogus inter Philosophum, Judaeum et Christianum*,

---

[20]Cf. P. Faider, *Études sur Sénèque*, I: *La gloire de Sénèque*; II: *La vie et l'oeuvre de Sénèque*; III: *La Vita Senecae par Paulus Pompilius* (Gand, 1921); Klaus-Dieter Nothdurft, *Studien zum Einfluss Senecas auf die Philosophie und Theologie des zwölften Jahrhunderts* (Leiden-Cologne, 1963); L.D. Reynolds, *The Medieval Tradition of Seneca's Letters* (Oxford, 1965).

[21]P. Faider, *Études sur Sénèque*, p. 135.

[22]*Entheticus*, vv. 1267–68 (*PL* 199, 992 C).

[23]John of Salisbury, *Policraticus*, VIII, 13, 763b–764a: Sunt tamen qui eum contempnere audeant, Quintiliani auctoritate freti (. . .) Mihi tamen desipere videntur qui quemcumque secuti non venerantur eum quem et Apostoli familiaritatem meruisse constat et a doctissimo Patre Ieronimo in sanctorum catalogo positum (763b).

[24]P. Faider, *Études sur Sénèque*, p. 137.

[25]*Policraticus*, VIII, 13, 764b: Ubique fidelis custos virtutis, ubique vitiorum hostis occurrit.

[26]*Fons philosophiae*, ed. P. Michaud-Quantin, Analecta Mediaevalia Namurcensia, 8 (Namur-Lille-Louvain, 1956), p. 49, vv. 411–12.

[27]*Anticlaudianus*, ed. R. Bossuat (Paris, 1955), p. 61; I, 135–36: More suo Seneca mores ratione monetat, optimus excultor morum mentisque colonus.

Peter Abelard calls Seneca the greatest of all moralists—a model of self-control.[28] Because of the high esteem Seneca enjoyed in the Middle Ages, many medieval thinkers refer to him in their writings and are influenced by his philosophy. By relying on investigations already completed and by limiting myself to a general survey without entering into details, I may mention the following authors. From the twelfth century, first of all, there is William of Conches. He is probably the author of the *Moralium dogma philosophorum*.[29] This work is dedicated to the young Prince Henry of Anjou-Plantagenet, who in 1154 became King Henry II of England. It is a synthesis of moral precepts borrowed in the main from Cicero's *De officiis* and from Seneca's *Letters* and his *De Beneficiis*. As has already been noted by Professor Delhaye, the author relies completely on the resources of human reason and quotes almost exclusively from writers foreign to Christian thinking.[30] He summarizes the goal he is pursuing in the following words: "to conform life to the norm of reason" (*ad normam rationis vitam reducere*).[31]

John of Salisbury refers several times in his *Policraticus* and *Metalogicon* to Seneca's authority in order to support his own teachings. In the *Policraticus* he refutes Quintilian's criticism of the Roman philosopher,[32] whereas in the *Metalogicon* he borrows from Seneca a famous definition of human reason: "a particle of the divine Spirit, implanted in a human body."[33] It must be noted,

---

[28]*Dialogus inter Philosophum, Judaeum et Christianum*, ed. R. Thomas (Stuttgart, 1970), p. 99, 1537-38: ille maximus morum edificator et continentissime (. . .) vite. Cf. *Epist.* VIII (*PL* 178, 297 B); *Epist.* XII (*PL* 178, 350 B).
[29]*Das Moralium Dogma Philosophorum des Guillaume de Conches*, ed. J. Holmberg (Uppsala, 1929), p. 7.
[30]Ph. Delhaye, "Une adaptation du *De Officiis* au XIIe siècle: le *Moralium Dogma Philosophorum*," *Recherches de Théologie ancienne et médiévale* 16 (1949), p. 233.
[31]*Moralium Dogma Philosophorum*, p. 72, 23.
[32]*Policraticus*, VIII, 13, 763b: the author quotes a long passage from *De Instit. orat.* of Quintilian (X, 1, §125-31).
[33]*Metalogicon*, ed. C. Webb (Oxford, 1929), IV, 16, 925d, p. 182, 18-19: Ratio est quaedam pars divini spiritus humanis immersa corporibus. Cf. Seneca, *Epist.* 66, 12: Ratio autem nihil aliud est quam in corpus humanum pars divini spiritus mersa.

however, that in John of Salisbury this definition has been completely freed of its pantheistic and materialistic implications.[34]

Abelard also refers to the Roman philosopher on several occasions. He quotes the *Proverbia Senecae*,[35] mentions the correspondence between Seneca and St. Paul,[36] and shows himself to be familiar with the *Letters to Lucilius* and the *De Beneficiis*.[37] Abelard definitely accepted two typically Stoic doctrines, that is, that virtue is universally human, and that moral life is a coherent unity.[38]

Alan of Lille takes his inspiration from the Roman philosopher in his *De arte praedicatoria*.[39] He even adopts Seneca's viewpoint by stating that the wise man can be happy by himself.[40] William of St. Thierry in his *Epistola aurea*—a letter addressed to the community of Mont-Dieu in 1145—also relies on Seneca's psychological teaching, but as interpreted in the sense of Christian spiritualism.[41] Moreover, he adopts the fundamental rule of moral life as it was formulated by the Stoics, that is, a life in agreement with nature, meaning thereby reason.[42] Within the same context I might mention Peter Cantor, who in his *Verbum abbreviatum* confers upon Seneca the title "Theologian" (*theologus*);[43] William of Malmesbury whose *Polyhistor* contains many quotations taken from the *Letters to*

---

[34]*Metalogicon*, IV, 16, 925d–926a.

[35]*Sic et non*, *PL* 178, 1589 A; *Sermo* XXX, *PL* 178, 567 A; *Sermo* XXXIII, *PL* 178, 590 C.

[36]*Sermo* XXIV, *PL* 178, 835 D; *In Epist. Pauli ad Romanos*, *PL* 178, 790 B–C; E.M. Buytaert, *Petri Abaelardi Opera Theologica*, I, p. 50, 109–51, 128 and *Theol. Scholarium*, I, 24 (*PL* 178, 1033 D).

[37]Abelard quotes *De beneficiis*, V, 6, 1–2, and *Epist.* 53 (in fact *Epist.* 51, 1–2) in his *Sermo* XXXIII and in his *Epist.* XII (*PL* 178, 592 A and 593 A; 350 B–C).

[38]*Dialogus inter Philosophum, Judaeum et Christianum*, pp. 88ff.

[39]*De arte praedicatoria*, c. 3 (*PL* 210, 117 D–118 A; 159 B–C).

[40]Seneca, *Epist.* 9, 13.

[41]*Un traité de la vie solitaire: Epistola ad fratres de Monte Dei, éd. et trad.* by M.M. Davy, Études de philosophie médiévale, 29, 1–2 (Paris, 1940); *Lettre d'or aux frères du Mont-Dieu, Introduction, traduction et notes* by J.M. Dechanet (Paris, 1956); J.M. Dechanet, "*Seneca noster*. Des Lettres à Lucilius à la Lettre aux frères du Mont-Dieu," in *Mélanges J. de Ghellinck*, II (Gembloux, 1951), pp. 753–66.

[42]"Le 'naturam sequi' chez Guillaume de Saint-Thierry," *Collectanea Ordinis Cisterciensium Reformatorum* 7 (1940–45), pp. 141–48.

[43]*Verbum abbreviatum*, *PL* 205, 25 A (cf. Seneca, *Epist.* 16, 7).

Lucilius;[44] and finally, Otho of Freising, who in his *Chronica* clearly reveals his familiarity with the work of the Roman philosopher.[45] Among thirteenth-century thinkers I must mention Roger Bacon, who has the undeniable merit of having introduced into his work the *Dialogues* of Seneca. In the third part of his *Moralis Philosophia* he quotes extensive extracts from this work by the Roman philosopher.[46] This is quite understandable since Bacon endeavors to unite into a coherent whole the ethics of the philosophers and the teaching of faith.[47] Although Bacon is a Christian, he greatly admires Seneca's thought and Aristotle's ethics.[48] Vincent of Beauvais, in his *De eruditione filiorum nobilium*, borrows about fifty quotations from Seneca.[49] References to the Roman philosopher are also quite frequent in Thomas of York's *Sapientiale*.[50] As regards Thomas Aquinas, in the *Summa Theologiae* (II-IIae) there are many quotations from Seneca (about forty explicit references). Thomas also refers to the *Liber de quattuor virtutibus*, which he regards as an authentic writing by the Stoic thinker.[51] William Perraut in his *De eruditione*

---

[44]*Polyhistor* is an unedited compilation of extracts taken from Christian and pagan authors. It has been preserved in two manuscripts: Harleianus 3969, ff. 25v-28v and Cambridge, St. John's College, D 22, ff. 192-95.

[45]*Chronica sive Historia de duabus civitatibus*, ed. altera, rec. A. Hofmeister, Scriptores rerum Germanicarum in usum scholarum (Hannover-Leipzig, 1912).

[46]*Moralis Philosophia*, ed. E. Massa (Zurich, 1953), pp. 73, 3-184, 9.

[47]*Op. cit.*, dist. 5, prooemium, pp. 132, 15-133, 7; *ibid.* p. 214, 16-17; p. 214, 24-26.

[48]Aristotle, whose *Ethics* is frequently quoted, is called "omnium philosophorum excellentissimus" (*op. cit.*, p. 28, 15). Referring to the third part of his exposition, in which the extracts from Seneca are particularly extensive, Bacon declares: Protraxi hanc partem terciam Moralis philosophie gratis propter pulcritudinem et utilitatem sententiarum moralium, et propter hoc quod libri raro inveniuntur, a quibus erui has morum radices et flores et fructus (*op. cit.*, p. 187, 1-4).

[49]*De Eruditione filiorum nobilium*, ed. A. Steiner, Mediaeval Academy of America Publications, 32 (Càmbridge, Mass., 1938); cf. L. Lieser, *Vinzenz von Beauvais als Kompilator und Philosoph*, Forschungen z. Gesch. d. Phil. u. Päd., 3 (Leipzig, 1928); *Martini Episcopi Bracarensis opera omnia*, ed. Cl. W. Barlow (New Haven, 1950), p. 208.

[50]A critical edition of this work is currently being prepared by J.R. O'Donnell (Toronto). Cf. also E. Longpré, "Fr. Thomas d'York, O.F.M. La première Somme métaphysique du XIIIe siècle," *Arch. Franc. Hist.* 19 (1926), pp. 875-930.

[51]*Summa Theologiae*, II-II, q. 129, a. 5, obj. 1; *ibid.*, ad 2.

principum—a work mistakenly attributed to Thomas Aquinas—frequently cites Seneca's writings.[52] The same is true of the *De principis instructione* of Giraldus Cambrensis,[53] and of Albertanus of Brescia's *Liber consolationis et consilii*.[54] William of Sherwood's *Syncategoremata* takes its inspiration from Stoic logic.[55] (The term *syncategorema* belongs to technical philosophical vocabulary and signifies a word that can be neither subject nor predicate in a sentence. Its meaning depends entirely upon the logical function it fulfills in a proposition.) The influence of Stoic logic is also to be discerned in Peter of Spain's *Summulae*.[56]

Among fourteenth-century authors the first to be mentioned is Barlaam of Seminara. He lived and lectured in the main in Greece, but in 1342 was present at the Pontifical Court at Avignon, where his friend Petrarch was his pupil. He is the author of a summary of Stoic moral philosophy, entitled *Ethica secundum Stoicos ex pluribus voluminibus eorumdem Stoicorum sub compendio composita*.[57] Presumably due to the influence of Barlaam's teaching, Petrarch often refers to Stoic philosophers and their views in his *De remediis utriusque fortunae*.[58] Nicholas Trivet, one of the best defenders and propagandists of Thomistic teaching at Oxford, is well known for

---

[52]Cf. A. Dondaine, "G. Peyraut, vie et oeuvre," *Arch. Fratrum Praed*. 18 (1948), pp. 162–236. Perraut frequently refers to Seneca. In the Vives Edition of Aquinas's works, the *De Eruditione principum* is found in vol. 37, pp. 551–673 (opusculum 37).

[53]*De principis instructione*, ed. G.F. Warner (London, 1891), *Giraldi Cambrensis opera* I–VIII, ed. J.S. Brewer, J.F. Dimock, G.F. Warner (London, 1861–1891), VIII.

[54]*Liber consolationis et consilii*, ed. Th. Sundby (London, 1873).

[55]"The Syncategoremata of William of Sherwood," ed. J.R. O'Donnell, *Mediaeval Studies* III (1941); *William of Sherwood's Treatise on Syncategorematic Words*, transl. with an introduction and notes by N. Kretzmann (Minneapolis, 1968; London, 1969).

[56]*Summulae logicales*, ed. J.P. Mullaly, Publications in Mediaeval Studies, VIII (Notre Dame, Indiana, 1945); *Petri Hispani Summulae Logicales quas e codice manuscripto Reg. Lat. 1205*, ed. I.M. Bochenski (Turin, 1947). Cf. also L.M. De Rijk, "On the Genuine Text of Peter of Spain's *Summulae logicales*," *Vivarium* 6 (1968), pp. 1–34, 69–101; 7 (1969), 8–61, 120–61; 8 (1970), 10–55; Peter of Spain, *Tractatus (Called afterwards "Summulae Logicales"), First Critical Edition from the Manuscripts with an Introduction* by L.M. De Rijk (Assen, 1972).

[57]*PG* 151, 1341–64.

[58]*De Remediis utriusque fortunae*, libri II (Venice, 1536).

his commentaries on works of Seneca,[59] including the *Declamationes Senecae* (written by Seneca the rhetor) and several tragedies. Meister Eckhart often quotes the *Letters to Lucilius* in his Commentary on the *Book of Wisdom*.[60] He congratulates the Stoics for having known that external goods contribute nothing to virtue or to a good and happy life.[61] In his *Consolatio Theologiae* John of Dambach often refers to Seneca's works.[62] We should note, however, that most of his citations probably come from the *Manipulus florum* of Thomas Hibernicus (a *socius* of the Sorbonne, who died before 1331).[63] To this list one may add the name of Nicholas Oresme, who in his book on Aristotle's *Politics* often quotes works of Seneca, including his *Letters, Dialogues, Quaestiones naturales, De Beneficiis*, and *Declamationes*.[64]

And yet this admiration for Seneca's thought is not shared by all. Hugh of St. Victor is openly hostile to Seneca, as he is to all pagan philosophers.[65] The same is true of Walther of St. Victor in his *Contra quattuor labyrinthos Franciae*.[66] In particular he takes to task the Roman philosopher's teaching on suicide.[67] In his view this Stoic should be read only by those capable of discerning what is right and what wrong, what valuable and what worthless.[68]

In addition to authentic works by Seneca, I must mention a treatise wrongly attributed to him by medieval thinkers, that is, the *Formula vitae honestae*, also entitled *De quattuor virtutibus*.[69] This

[59]Cf. P. Glorieux, *La Faculté des arts et ses maîtres au XIIIe siècle* (Paris, 1971), pp. 263–66.
[60]This work has been edited by G. Thiry, *Arch. hist. doctr. litt. M.A.*, t. 3 (1928), pp. 321–443; t. 4 (1929), pp. 233–394.
[61]*Op. cit.*, t. 3, p. 438.
[62]Cf. A. Auer, "Johannes von Dambach und die Trostbücher vom 11. bis zum 16. Jahrhundert," *Beiträge zur Geschichte der Philosophie und Theologie des M.A.* 14 (Münster, 1928), pp. 78–96; pp. 108–56.
[63]Cf. R.H. Rouse, "The List of Authorities appended to the *Manipulus Florum*," *Arch. hist. doctr. litt. M.A.* 32 (1966), pp. 243–50.
[64]Ed. A. Douglas Menut (Philadelphia, 1970).
[65]*Didascalion*, ed. G. Buttimer (Washington, 1939), p. 70, 13–16 (*PL* 176, 1777 C–D).
[66]Ed. P. Glorieux, *Arch. hist. doctr. litt. M.A.* 19 (1952), pp. 187–335.
[67]*Op. cit.*, IV, 2, p. 270, 30; cf. Ph. Delhaye, *Le microcosme de Godefroi de Saint-Victor* (Lille, 1951), II: *Étude théologique*, p. 31 and p. 245.
[68]*Op. cit.*, p. 272, 25.
[69]*Martini Episcopi Bracarensis opera omnia*, ed. Cl. Barlow (New Haven, 1950), pp. 204–50.

work was written by a Spanish bishop in the sixth century, Martin of Bracara (+580).[70] It was composed of extracts borrowed from a lost treatise by Seneca, probably his *De officiis*.[71] Moreover, there is the *De copia verborum*, a mutilated version of the *Formula*, to which several extracts from Letters 1 to 88 have been joined.[72]

Owing to the study of certain manuscripts we now know that already in the early Middle Ages florilegia containing extracts from Seneca were composed. For instance, the *Florilegium Gallicum* has been preserved in five manuscripts and contains many passages from Seneca's *Letters* (until Letter 88).[73] In addition, there are the *Proverbia Senecae*,[74] quoted among others by Abelard in his *Sic et non*.[75] Mention should also be made of the Roman philosopher's *Monita*.[76] According to J. Haes some of these *Monita* may be found literally in Seneca's works. Others are simply in agreement with his thought; and still others may be attributed to him for stylistic reasons.[77] As to the *Liber de moribus*,[78] it was probably drawn from the *Monita* and contains a collection of 145 sentences.[79] Finally, the *Proverbia Senecae* were later joined to a collection of extracts from Aristotle under the title *Auctoritates Aristotelis*. There one can find several extracts taken from the *Formula vitae honestae* and the *Liber de moribus*.[80]

For medieval authors Seneca definitely is their main source for Stoic doctrines. In addition to Seneca there is Cicero, whose writ-

---

[70]*Op. cit.*, p. 7 and p. 208; cf. L.D. Reynolds, *The Medieval Tradition of Seneca's Letters*, p. 112.
[71]*Martini Episcopi Bracarensis opera omnia*, pp. 205-8.
[72]*Op. cit.*, pp. 208-10.
[73]A. Gagner, *Florilegium Gallicum. Untersuchungen und Texte zur Geschichte der mittellateinischen Florilegienliteratur* (Lund, 1936); cf. L.D. Reynolds, *The Medieval Tradition*, p. 121.
[74]In the codex *Vat. Regin. lat.* 1870, f. 1, the following indication may be found: Excerpta Senecae et sententiae morales seu proverbia.
[75]*PL* 178, 1589 A.
[76]L.A. *Senecae monita et eiusdem morientis extremae voces*, ed. E. Wölfflin, Progr. acad. 4 (Erlangen, 1978).
[77]*De L.A. Senecae Philosophi Monitis* (Würzburg, 1878), p. 21.
[78]*De Moribus*, ed. E. Wölfflin, in *Publilii Syri sententiae* (Leipzig, 1869), pp. 136-48; Seneca, *Opera*, ed. Haase, III, pp. 462-67.
[79]K.-D. Nothdurft, *op. cit.*, p. 32.
[80]Cf. J. Hamesse, "Auctoritates Aristotelis," doctoral thesis (Louvain, 1970), II, pp. 189ff.

ings are filled with Stoic ideas, especially in the field of ethics.[81] His works were read and studied during the Middle Ages and, as a consequence, their influence was considerable.[82] Consider, for instance, his *De officiis*. This work takes its inspiration from one of the main representatives of Middle Stoicism, Panaetius. With the help of Cicero's treatise, therefore, medieval readers were introduced to the thought of this Stoic philosopher. Hence the question should be raised: to what extent did Cicero's philosophical writings influence the thought of medieval philosophers and theologians? With respect to St. Augustine, this question has been investigated by Testard[83] and by H. Hagendahl.[84] In a recent article Ch. Baguette attempts to show that Augustine, having been nourished by reading Cicero's *De natura deorum* and before he came into contact with the work of Plotinus, passed through a Stoic stage.[85] The same kind of research must be applied to many other medieval writers. Any such study cannot, of course, be limited to a collection of literal quotations. It must recognize doctrinal influences in order to uncover the perhaps indirect penetration of the Stoic legacy into medieval civilization. As regards Thomas Aquinas, some years ago E.K. Rand directed a small study to references to Cicero which he found in the *Summa Theologiae*.[86] He notes that Aquinas often refers to Cicero

---

[81]P. Milton-Valente, *L'Ethique stoïcienne chez Cicéron* (Paris-Porto Alegre, no date).

[82]H. Baron, "Cicero and the Roman Civic Spirit in the Middle Ages and the Early Renaissance," *Bull. John Rylands Libr.* 22 (1938), pp. 72–97; P. Courcelle, "La postérité chrétienne du Sage de Scipion," *Revue Et. Lat.* 36 (1958), pp. 205–34; M. Dickly, "Some Commentaries on the *De Inventione* and *Ad Herennium* of the Eleventh and Early Twelfth Centuries," *Med. Ren. Studies* 8 (1968), pp. 1–42; G. Gawlick, "Cicero in der Patristik," in *Studia Patristica*, ed. F.L. Cross (Berlin, 1966). Studying the influence of Cicero on later generations with respect to Stoic anthropology, E. von Ivanka came to the conclusion that some later Latin authors, like Lactantius and St. Ambrose, not only reproduced the teaching of Cicero, but also had recourse to other sources, even those which had been utilized by Cicero himself ("Die stoische Anthropologie in der lateinischen Literatur," *Anzeiger Oesterr. Ak. Wissenschaften, Phil.-hist. Kl.* LXXXVII [1950], pp. 178–92).

[83]*Saint Augustin et Cicéron*, 2 vols. (Paris, 1958).

[84]*Augustine and the Latin Classics*, 2 vols. (Göteborg, 1967).

[85]"Une période stoïcienne dans l'évolution de la pensée de saint Augustin," *Revue Et. Aug.* 16 (1970), pp. 47–77.

[86]*Cicero in the Courtroom of St. Thomas Aquinas* (Milwaukee, 1946).

when dealing with virtues, and particularly to his *De inventione*. In Aquinas's view this work represents a little Gospel.[87] Thomas refers to it seventy times and never opposes its teaching. A general survey by C. Van Steenkiste on Aquinas's usage of Cicero shows that he frequently refers to this classical author. Not all of these references, of course, are to Stoic doctrines. This issue must be examined in each particular case.[88]

In addition to Cicero, medieval writers could find substantial information about Stoic thought in Calcidius's Commentary on Plato's *Timaeus*.[89] In a recent monograph, J. Den Boeft has shown that Calcidius, while wishing to maintain the Platonic teaching on fate, systematically criticizes the Stoic position on the same subject.[90]

As regards Boethius, according to F. Sassen he was "the master of the Middle Ages."[91] Due to P. Courcelle's remarkable studies we now realize how much Boethius's work, and in particular his *De consolatione philosophiae*, meant for later generations.[92] It is true that Boethius is far from being a Stoic; but when he criticizes certain Stoic positions, he cannot avoid presenting the doctrines he attempts to refute. Moreover, when he opposes the Stoics, as he so often does, this does not imply that he himself is completely free from their influence. Does not his definition of philosophy as "the science of human and divine things" clearly bear the stamp of the Stoic schools?[93]

Within this context I must single out a Latin translation, probably by Grosseteste, of a collection of definitions which manifest typical characteristics of Stoic philosophy, that is to say, the *De Passionibus*.[94] This work presents in turn the definitions and classifi-

---

[87]E.K. Rand, *op. cit.*, p. 44.
[88]"Cicerone nell'opera di S. Tommaso," *Angelicum* 36 (1959), pp. 343–82.
[89]*Timaeus a Calcidio translatus commentarioque instructus*, ed. J.H. Waszink (London-Leiden, 1952).
[90]*Calcidius on Fate. His Doctrine and Sources* (Leiden, 1970).
[91]"Boëthius, Leermeester der Middeleeuwen," *Stud. Cath.* 14 (1938), pp. 97–122; pp. 216–30.
[92]*La consolation de la philosophie dans la tradition littéraire. Antécédents et postérité de Boèce*, Études Augustiniennes (1967).
[93]*De Philosophiae consolatione*, ed. L. Bieler, Corpus Christianorum, Series latina, vol. XCIV (Turnhout, 1957), I, 4, p. 7, 9–10.
[94]*Pseudo-Andronicus de Rhodes, "Περὶ παθῶν", édition critique du texte grec et de la traduction médiévale*, by A. Glibert-Thirry, Corpus latinum commentariorum in Aristotelem graecorum, Suppl. 2 (Leiden, 1977); cf. L.

cation of passions, and then the definitions and classification of virtues. The text treating of passions is divided into two chapters. The first deals with the passions themselves, whereas the second studies the εὐπάθειαι, the good passions. In his discussion of virtues and vices, the author almost completely reproduces the pseudo-Aristotelian treatise *De virtutibus et vitiis*;[95] but he adds some definitions of virtues borrowed from a different source and considerably modifies the plan of the work. This pamphlet is frequently quoted, for instance, by Thomas Aquinas.[96] While it presents itself as a collection of definitions of Peripatetic origin, it actually introduced into medieval thought some Stoic doctrines under the cover of Aristotle.

On the other hand, those commentators on Aristotle whose works were partly translated into Latin during the thirteenth century also transmitted some Stoic doctrines to medieval thinkers. As an example one may mention Alexander of Aphrodisias's *De Fato*, which was translated by William of Moerbeke. Here a solution is presented for the problem of fatalism and freedom that combines Aristotelianism and Stoicism.[97] One may also cite commentators such as Aspasius and Simplicius. As has already been mentioned, the latter's Commentary on Aristotle's *Categories* provides valuable information concerning Stoic philosophy.[98] It is well known that Sextus Empiricus's writings offer many indications about Stoic thought. When one turns to the fragments of the ancient Stoic school as edited by J. von Arnim, one immediately realizes Sextus's importance in this respect.[99] One of these works, the πυρρωνείων

Tropia, "La versione latina medievale del περὶ παθῶν del Pseudo-Andronico," *Aevum* 26 (1952), pp. 97–112.

[95]A. Pelzer, "Les versions latines des ouvrages de morale conservés sous le nom d'Aristote en usage au XIIIe siècle," *Revue Néo-Scolastique de philosophie* 23 (1921), pp. 322ff.; cf. D.A. Callus, "Robert Grosseteste as Scholar," in *Robert Grosseteste, Scholar and Bishop*, ed. by D.A. Callus (Oxford, 1955), p. 64.

[96]Cf. G. Verbeke, "Saint Thomas et le Stoïcisme," in *Miscellanea Mediaevalia* (Berlin, 1962), pp. 47–68.

[97]G. Verbeke, "Aristotélisme et Stoïcisme dans le *De Fato* d'Alexandre d'Aphrodisias," *Arch. f. Gesch. Philos.* 50 (1968), pp. 73–100.

[98]Simplicius, *Commentaire sur les Catégories d'Aristote, traduction de Guillaume de Moerbeke*, ed. A. Pattin, Corpus latinum commentariorum in Aristotelem graecorum, V, 1 (Louvain-Paris, 1971).

[99]*Stoicorum Veterum Fragmenta*, 4 vols. (Stuttgart, 1903, 1905, 1924).

ὑποτυπώσεων, was translated into Latin in the thirteenth century under the title *Pirronie informationes*. The text has been preserved in a small number of manuscripts. This shows that it was not widely known.[100]
Finally, there were Arab philosophers whose works were translated into Latin. They also present some Stoic doctrines, coming frequently from the *Enchiridion* of Epictetus, the Greek Commentaries on Aristotle, Galen, and the *De Placitis* of Pseudo-Plutarch.[101] Many years ago M.-D. Chenu offered a striking example of Stoic[102] influence as transmitted through Arab philosophers. This has to do with Thomas Aquinas's usage of the term *imaginatio* to refer to simple apprehension (*simplex apprehensio*), and the term *fides* or *credulitas* to signify judgment. The first term (simple apprehension) corresponds to the Stoic φαντασία, whereas the second is a translation of the technical term συγκατάθεσις. The Arabic terminology was introduced into the West by Gundissalinus, one of the translators of Avicenna. Costa ben Luca (864–923), a Christian physician from Baalbek in Syria, is the author of a treatise dealing with the difference between soul and spirit. This work was translated into Latin by John of Spain under the title *De differentia inter animam et spiritum*. Its author distinguishes between two kinds of spirits. The first comes from the heart, the principle of life and respiration. The second springs from the brain, spreads through the nerves, and is the cause of movement and sensation. The Stoics are known to have regarded the soul as a material breath. Costa ben Luca cate-

---

[100]*Pyrrhoniarum informationum libri III*: the text has been preserved in a Paris manuscript, originating from St. Victor Abbey (Paris. lat. 14700).

[101]Cf. O. Amin, *Le Stoïcisme chez les Arabes* [in Arabic] (Cairo, 1945); "Le Stoïcisme et la pensée islamique," *Bull. of the Faculty of Arts*, 17 (Cairo University) (1955), pp. 13–14; "Le Stoïcisme et la pensée musulmane," *Revue Thomiste* 59 (1959), pp. 79–97; F. Jadaane, *L'influence du Stoïcisme sur la pensée musulmane*, Recherches publiées sous la direction de l'Institut de Lettres Orientales de Beyrouth, Série I: Pensée arabe et musulmane, XLI (Beirut, 1968); S. Gomez Nogales, "Le Stoïcisme dans la philosophie musulmane" (Ve Congrès international d'arabisants et d'islamisants, Bruxelles, 1970; Brussels, no date).

[102]"Un vestige du Stoïcisme," *Rev. Sc. Philos. et Théol.* 27 (1938), pp. 63–68; cf. H.A. Wolfson, "The Terms of *tasawwur* and *tasdīq* in Arabic Philosophy and their Greek, Latin and Hebrew Equivalents," *The Moslem World* (1943), pp. 114–28; Ibn Sina, *Livres des directives et remarques*, traduction avec Introduction et Notes by A.-M. Goichon (Beirut-Paris, 1951), p. 81.

gorically rejects any materialistic conception of the soul, but he attacks this position without formally attributing it to the Stoics. According to him, spirit is an intermediary between soul and body. A similar position appears in Avicenna and will be taken up by some medieval thinkers in the West.[103] The distinction between soul and spirit is also found in Isaac Israeli's *De definitionibus*.

From this general survey we may already conclude that the presence of Stoicism in medieval thought cannot be studied in the same way as the influence of Aristotelianism. In the latter case we have to rely in the main on the translations of particular treatises and their penetration into University life and teaching. During the Middle Ages countless commentaries on particular Aristotelian treatises were written. These clearly indicate how these texts were studied and explained, again and again, in all European centers of higher learning. As regards Stoicism, one must rather look for explicit quotations from Stoic sources, for expositions of Stoic doctrines, and for critical examinations of Stoic viewpoints whether favorable or unfavorable. But the most decisive approach will undoubtedly seek to discover typical Stoic topics and themes which were handed down from antiquity and gradually incorporated into the heritage of Western thought. This is not to imply that Stoic philosophy was uncritically accepted. In fact, it was partly accepted and partly rejected. But even in those cases where it was opposed, it must be carefully examined, since both opposition and assimilation point to the presence of Stoicism in medieval thought.

[103]Thomas Aquinas, *Summa Theologiae*, I, q. 76, a. 7, ad 2.

CHAPTER II

THE CHALLENGE OF MATERIALISM

Materialism is a rather vague and ambiguous term. It is applied to various philosophical systems which differ greatly from one another in inspiration and fundamental intuition. Can we say that the first philosophical system in Western thought was materialistic because Thales of Miletus regarded water as the ultimate element of which everything is composed? One would be mistaken to draw such a conclusion, since Thales never formally considered spiritualism and materialism as alternative choices. In other words, he never repudiated spiritualism and consciously decided for materialism. This qualification must be kept in mind, especially when one is dealing with ancient Greek philosophers or, for that matter, even with later representatives of Western thought. Thales did not distinguish clearly between living beings and inorganic matter, even as he did not clearly realize that some reality may be incorporeal. In this sense, his philosophy is not a formal and conscious materialism.

Even within the framework of ancient philosophy materialism does not always have the same meaning. Epicureanism and Stoicism both belong to the Hellenistic period. Both are regarded as materialistic, and yet their explanations of the universe are far from identical. Epicurus wanted to account for the variety of beings and their manifestations by reducing them to two fundamental components: atoms, which differ only quantitatively from one another; and empty space. His main concern was to reduce, insofar as possible, multiplicity and change to some fundamental identity, by holding that everything is made of the same components. What exists from eternity will also remain in the future. Only the combinations of atoms change. His is a world of identity. History is reduced to a minimum. This perspective could hardly be found in Stoicism. What the Stoics aim at is a coherent and optimistic interpretation of reality. In their view, being is not the highest category under which everything is included. Only corporeal things may be called beings, because they alone are active and capable of producing or performing something.¹ What is not corporeal is incapable of realizing anything. The world as a whole and the various things that exist within it develop and grow out of an initial seed in which all the features that will later appear are already present in seminal fashion. The evolution of the cosmos, being like that of an organism, is understood after the manner of a biological process which gradually manifests certain hidden possibilities. Everything is conceived according to the pattern of embryological growth. The initial seeds are corporeal and their growth is that of a corporeal reality. Hence one can readily understand why, according to Stoicism, if things are to be active they must be corporeal. Even the highest principle, immanent spirit or World-Soul, cannot be incorporeal. Being present everywhere, it constantly makes the world a perfect animated organism. Whatever happens in the world must be seen in light of the totality. With respect to this, the Stoics had to face a difficult problem. If the divine principle is present everywhere, like a soul permeating every part of a body, is this not to imply that two bodies exist in the same place? The Stoics tried to resolve this problem by appealing to the idea of total penetration or amalgamation, but this solution has frequently been criticized.²

According to the Stoic school, the highest category is not being but "something" (*quid*). This notion is broader in extension than being. While being coincides with the corporeal, "something" also includes incorporeal objects such as time, space, the void, and what

---

¹Sextus, *Adv. math.*, VIII, 263 (*SVF* II, 363). According to the Stoics the highest category is "something" (*quid* in the translation of Seneca; τό τι), which includes the incorporeal as well as the corporeal. Alexander of Aphrodisias (*Comm. in Arist. Topica*, IV, p. 155 Ald., p. 301, 19 Wal. [*SVF* II, 325]) wonders whether the notion of something really includes whatever exists. Therefore he compares "something" to the notion of unity and one. The latter may also be attributed to concepts. It may be right to state that a concept is one. Is it also something? Not according to the Stoic vocabulary, since a concept is neither corporeal nor incorporeal. As a matter of fact, it is not listed among the incorporeals. It is easy, however, to suspect the reply of the Stoics. In their view a concept is always connected with the notion of *lekton*, for the content of an expressible is a concept. In this sense, the expressible is an intermediary between a concept and reality (Ammonius, *In Arist. De interpr.*, p. 17, 24 [*SVF* II, 168]). A concept as well as an expressible is an incorporeal.

²Alexander Aphrod., *De mixtione*, p. 224, 32 Bruns (*SVF* II, 310).

The Challenge of Materialism 23

is called *lekton*, the "expressible."³ This last-mentioned notion plays an important role in the Stoic theory of knowledge. When a sensible image becomes an "expressible" object, knowledge proceeds to the intellectual level. These incorporeals are not beings. They are unable to produce anything. Of these, space, time, and the void are a kind of open receptacle in which the development of beings takes place.⁴ Neither space nor time affects beings in what they are. Time is not an active principle either of progress or of decay. The "expressible" is also unable to do anything. When the content of experience is expressed in human language, nothing is changed by this verbal translation—neither the content of sensible experience nor the external world. Hence, the intuition that dominates Stoic materialism is its firm conviction that causation always implies corporeity.

It is remarkable that a Christian writer such as Tertullian adopted Stoic materialism without hesitation, even though he did not accept the coincidence of human soul and divine Spirit. Individual soul is not, according to Tertullian, a particle of immanent divine Reason.⁵ Emphasizing a distinction between God and man, he calls the divine substance *spiritus*, a term that corresponds to the Stoic *pneuma*. He terms the soul *flatus* (breath).⁶ The relation between the two is comparable to that between wind and breeze. There is affinity between the two principles, with the latter being dependent upon the former.⁷ Another comparison used by Tertullian is that of a pattern and a copy. Human soul is a copy of the divine perfection, and realizes the fullness of this perfection in a limited way.⁸ He also

---

³Sextus, *Adv. math.*, X, 218 (*SVF* II, 321).

⁴Alexander Aphrod., *Comm. in Arist. Topica*, IV, p. 155 Ald., p. 301, 19 Wal. (*SVF* II, 329). The author maintains that "something" necessarily implies being. Seneca (*Epist.* 58, 12) states that "quod est" is the most general category. He does not agree with the Stoics who want to introduce a more universal notion, namely "something." They were brought to this opinion, because people form certain images to which no reality corresponds—sheer fantasies, like centaurs or giants (*Epist.* 58, 15). Hence they believed that centaurs could not belong to the category of "quod est."

⁵F. Seyr, *Die Seelen- und Erkenntnislehre Tertullians und die Stoa*, Commentationes Vindobonenses, III (1937), p. 52.

⁶*De res. mortuorum*, 7, 8, ed. Borleffs (Corpus Christianorum, II, p. 930): spiritus sui auram, oris sui operam . . .; *Adv. Marc.*, II, 9 (the whole chapter), ed. Aem. Kroymann (Corp. Christ., I, p. 484).

⁷*Adv. Marc.*, II, 9, ed. Kroymann (Corp. Christ., I, p. 484).

⁸*Adv. Marc.*, II, 9, ed. Kroymann (Corp. Christ., I, p. 485).

compares the relation between God and human soul to that of a potter and his product. The product has been produced by a craftsman and bears the characteristics of his mind, but without belonging to the same level of perfection.[9] God is eternal, while human soul, though immortal, comes into being. For this reason human soul is not impassible and does not enjoy imperturbable happiness.[10]

This view of Tertullian obviously differs from that of the apologist Tatian. This writer regards human soul as a material *pneuma*, but also admits in addition to this material principle a supersensible immaterial *pneuma*. Thinking within the framework of Stoic categories, Tertullian could hardly admit that God is incorporeal. That would mean that God is comparable to time, space, and the other incorporeals, and without any activity or creative power.[11] When Tertullian maintains that God is corporeal, he does not wish to say that the divine Being is on the same level as the sensible world, but rather that God is not a mere abstraction. God is a real substance, the source of a constant creative activity. According to Tertullian, everything that exists is corporeal. It is a *corpus sui generis*. Hence the reality of the divine Being implies that he is corporeal.[12]

As regards the nature of the human soul, which in its corporeal structure is similar to that of the body, Tertullian is mainly opposed to the teaching of the Gnostics.[13] According to them, the soul is a spark of the divine substance. As the result of a fall, it has been imprisoned within the body. It constantly strives to free itself and to return to its origin. The Gnostics regard the world as essentially evil. The cosmos is not the work of God but of a lower power, which does not even know the divine Principle. Tertullian always rejected this pessimistic doctrine. He stresses the connatural relationship between body and soul, and rejects the Gnostic view that life on

[9] *Adv. Marc.*, II, 9, ed. Kroymann (Corp. Christ., I, p. 485).
[10] *De Anima*, 24, ed. J.H. Waszink (Corp. Christ., II, p. 816).
[11] *De carne Christi*, 11, ed. Kroymann (Corp. Christ., II, p. 895): Omne, quod est, corpus est sui generis, nihil est incorporale, nisi quod non est; *Adv. Hermog.*, 35, ed. Kroymann (Corp. Christ., I, p. 427): Cum ipsa substantia corpus sit rei cuiusque; *De An.*, 7, ed. Waszink (Corp. Christ., II, p. 790): Nihil enim, si non corpus.
[12] *Adv. Prax.*, 7, ed. Kroymann et E. Evans (Corp. Christ., II, p. 1166): Quis negabit Deum corpus esse, etsi Deus spiritus est? Spiritus enim corpus sui generis in sua effigie.
[13] *De res. mortuorum*, 17, ed. Borleffs (Corp. Christ., II, p. 941); *De Anima*, 8-9, ed. Waszink (Corp. Christ., II, pp. 759-60).

earth is an exile and that man's only salvation consists in freeing himself from the body. In order to establish the corporeal character of the soul, Tertullian has recourse to Stoic arguments, which point mainly to the interaction between body and soul. He also refers to Christian teaching concerning the destiny of souls after death. Some are punished in hell or in purgatory; but this would be impossible if they were incorporeal.[14] Although it is a material breath, the human soul is nonetheless uncomposed, indivisible, and immortal. After death it continues to exist and can never be dissolved.[15]

In considering the origin of our psychic principle, Tertullian refuses to admit that it comes from without.[16] Here again he agrees with the Stoic view that the souls of children, like their bodies, stem from their parents.[17] Hence he distinguishes two kinds of seeds, a *semen corporale*, which is a part of the body of the parents, and a *semen animale*, which is a particle of their soul. This doctrine corresponds to Stoic traducianism, which points to resemblance between parents and children not only with respect to their body but also with respect to their psychic character. Tertullian also develops this position in order to account for the transmission of original sin.[18] Tertullian's materialism is obviously inspired by Stoicism, but is at the same time a reaction on his part against Gnostic pessimism.

A century after Tertullian, at the end of the third century and the beginning of the fourth, Lactantius appears as another representative of this materialistic trend. He maintains that the human soul is a subtle and imperceptible breath that, while not totally impassible, is nonetheless immortal.[19] In agreement with Tertullian, he also holds that the divine substance is "spiritual," meaning thereby that it is a corporeal spirit—a fine and warm breath. Whereas Tertullian

---

[14]*De Anima*, 7, ed. Waszink (Corp. Christ., II, p. 790).
[15]*De Anima*, 14, ed. Waszink (Corp. Christ., II, p. 799): Itaque quia non mortalis, neque dissolubilis, neque divisibilis. Nam et dividi dissolvi est et dissolvi mori est.
[16]*De Anima*, 25, ed. Waszink (Corp. Christ., II, pp. 819-21).
[17]*De Anima*, 27, ed. Waszink (Corp. Christ., II, pp. 822-24).
[18]G. Verbeke, *L'Evolution de la doctrine du pneuma du Stoïcisme à S. Augustin* (Paris-Louvain, 1945), pp. 448-49.
[19]*Divinae Institutiones*, ed. S. Brandt, p. 650, 23: Quod ergo mirum, si cum sint immortales animae, tamen patibiles sint Deo? Nam cum in se nihil habeant solidum et contrectabile, a solidis et corporalibus nullam vim pati possunt; sed quia in solis spiritibus vivunt, a solo Deo tractabiles sunt, cui virtus et substantia spiritalis est.

reserves the name *spiritus* for the divine substance alone, Lactantius does not make this distinction in terminology. He uses the same word to indicate the nature of God and that of the human soul, although he does not admit that the soul is an ἀπόσπασμα or a particle of the divine substance. On this issue he fully agrees with Tertullian, his predecessor.[20]

According to Lactantius it is not only divine substance that is spiritual or pneumatic, but also its power. By means of his powerful breath God acts within the sensible world and governs the whole of creation. Lactantius states that the wonderful harmony of the cosmos has been planned by God's providence, effected by his creative power, completed by his thought, preserved by his spirit, and governed by his almighty hand. Thus Lactantius uses the term *spiritus* to designate one of the many aspects of divine activity.[21] The divine breath exercises its action throughout the cosmos. Not a single spot in the universe can escape from its influence. Because the spirit of God permeates the entire world and is present everywhere, it is useless to make statues or images of God.[22] When the earth seems to produce animals, this is nothing but an illusion on the part of those who consider only the appearances of things. In fact it is the divine spirit, diffused throughout the world, that produces life and knowledge everywhere.[23] One might expect Lactantius to conclude that a part of this divine breath is present in each being and animates it. However, he does not draw this conclusion. Human soul and the vital principle of other living beings are not regarded as particles of the material and omnipresent divinity.

According to Lactantius not only is God's nature spiritual, but so, too, is that of angels and the human soul. In dealing with the last-mentioned point, Lactantius maintains that man results from the harmonious union of two opposed elements—water and fire. After having shaped man's body, God introduced into it a breath that comes from the vital source of his eternal spirit. In this way man is an image of the world in which he has to live, and which itself is also

---

[20]R. Pichon, *Lactance* (Paris, 1901), p. 99.
[21]*Divinae Institutiones*, ed. S. Brandt, p. 29, 5.
[22]*Divinae Institutiones*, ed. S. Brandt, p. 100, 10: Et tamen hominis imago necessaria tum videtur, cum procul abest, supervacua futura, cum praesto est, dei autem, cujus numen et spiritus ubique diffusus abesse numquam potest, semper utique supervacua est.
[23]*Divinae Institutiones*, ed. S. Brandt, p. 136, 10.

a combination of contrary components.²⁴ This conception is obviously based on the biblical narrative of man's creation, interpreted in a materialistic way. Lactantius takes the notion of *spiritus* in the sense of the Stoic πνεῦμα, but without identifying the divine substance with human soul. This common spiritual nature is the ground for kinship between God and man, as well as the basis for universal brotherhood among all human beings, whatever their bodily differences may be.²⁵ In spite of this materialism, Lactantius uses the same dualistic expressions one finds in Seneca's writings. The body is the temporary dwelling place of a celestial spirit. This spirit constantly strives to free itself and to return to its eternal destiny.²⁶

Owing to the influence of Cicero and Seneca, Lactantius has almost unconsciously interpreted biblical texts in the light of Stoic materialism. This same trend is found in the works of Macarius of Egypt, a mystical writer of the fourth century. He also maintains that human soul, angels, and evil demons are corporeal. Although they are subtle breaths, they still subsist in their own right and have their own specific form as do solid bodies.²⁷ God, however, whose transcendent character Macarius strongly emphasizes, escapes from this universal materialism. Given this, God decided to assume a body so that he might enter into contact with his sensible creatures such as the souls of saints and angels, and thus make them participate in divine life.²⁸

Plotinus began to develop his teaching in Rome in 245. His philosophy is highly spiritualistic and exercised deep influence on Western thought. Like the Christians, he strongly opposed Gnosticism.²⁹ His best-known and most gifted disciple, Porphyry, was

---

²⁴*Divinae Institutiones*, ed. S. Brandt, p. 155, 10: In ipsius autem hominis fictione illarum duarum materiarum, quas inter se diximus esse contrarias, ignis et aquae, conclusit perfecitque rationem. Ficto enim corpore, inspiravit ei animam de vitali fonte spiritus sui qui est perennis, ut ipsius mundi ex contrariis constantis elementis similitudinem gereret (*ibid.*, p. 735, 11).

²⁵*Divinae Institutiones*, ed. S. Brandt, p. 650, 23; p. 447, 24: Nam cum omnia humana non corpore sed spiritu metiamur, tametsi corporum sit diversa condicio, nobis tamen servi non sunt, sed eos et habemus et dicimus spiritu fratres, religione conservos.

²⁶*Divinae Institutiones*, ed. S. Brandt, p. 157, 9.

²⁷Macarius, *Homilia* IV, 9, *PG* 31, 480; IV, 10, *PG* 31, 480.

²⁸Macarius, *Homilia* IV, 9, *PG* 31, 480.

²⁹In 263 Plotinus finally decided to compose a treatise against the Gnos-

opposed to the Christians. Like many other intellectuals, he wanted to preserve intact the legacy of Hellenic tradition and culture. In light of this development, it is quite clear that as late as the fourth century, due to the influence of Stoic philosophy, attempts were still being made to interpret the Christian message in a materialistic way.

Saint Augustine is rightly called the teacher of the Middle Ages. Many medieval authors refer to his writings as documents endowed with exceptional authority in philosophy and theology. Before he came into contact with the spiritualism of Plotinus, Augustine had been influenced by other intellectual currents such as skepticism and Manichaeism. He also passed through a stage in which he was deeply touched by Stoic materialism.

In his *Confessions* he states that at a certain point in his development he regarded God as an immense power which pervades the entire universe, without being encompassed by the material world. According to this view, the divine principle permeates the entire sensible world. This principle is present in every part of it without being obstructed by anything, like sunlight which penetrates the air without tearing it to pieces or disrupting its unity. Augustine believed that the hidden divine breath governs everything that was created.[30] Although it is true that Plotinus also held the world to be penetrated by an immanent soul,[31] the doctrine to which Augustine refers in the *Confessions* cannot be Neoplatonism, since it is so clearly materialistic. God is viewed as a material breath, which permeates the universe and is diffused in all bodies in proportion to the space they occupy.[32] Such a materialistic conception is obviously at odds with the spiritualism of Plotinus. Moreover, the Neoplatonists do not admit that the world-soul is God, the highest principle of all that exists. Beyond the world-soul there are the principal hypostases which represent the highest levels of reality—the One, Intellect, and Universal Soul.[33] Finally, the general context wherein Augustine

---

tics who from the very beginning of his teaching in Rome were members of his school. In the Porphyry edition of Plotinus's works the treatise against the Gnostics has been split into four parts: III, 8; V, 8; V, 5; II, 9. Cf. Plotino, *Paideia antignostica. Introduzione e commento* by Vicenzo Cilento (Florence, 1971).

[30] *Confessiones*, VII, 1, 2.
[31] *Enn.*, IV, 4, 36.
[32] *Confessiones*, VII, 1, 2.
[33] *Enn.*, III, 5, 3.

presents this teaching clearly points to an earlier stage in his intellectual development, prior to his first contact with Victorinus's translations of Plotinus. Even Augustine's vocabulary manifests Stoic influence. To refer to God as an immanent material breath which governs everything from within corresponds to Stoic teaching.[34]

In his *De immortalitate animae* Augustine still believes that the world is animated. He states that every body exists by the soul that animates it, and he applies this to the cosmos as well as to any animated body located within it. In his *Retractations* Augustine comments that this entire passage was written rashly.[35] It is true that Plato and many other philosophers had viewed the world as a living organism. But, remarks Augustine, no philosopher has ever adequately proved that the world is animated, nor does Holy Scripture unequivocally teach this. Hence it is impossible either to assert this or to deny it. It is in this sense that he regarded his earlier remark in the *De immortalitate animae* as rash.[36]

Not only was Augustine well informed about Stoic teaching concerning the immanent divine Principle; he also had to face this school's position on the origin and nature of individual human souls. In one of his letters (no. 166) he replies to a question that had been submitted to him—whether human soul is a particle of the divine substance. This question fully reflects constant Stoic teaching. Augustine's reaction is completely negative. God is immutable in the highest degree. If the soul were a particle of divine substance, it would also be immutable and could undergo no change. In fact, however, we notice that the soul changes for better or for worse. Hence, it cannot be a particle of God. To counter that the change of the soul springs from the body will not solve the problem. If the soul changes under the influence of the body, it is not really immutable.[37]

Stoic influence is also evident in Augustine's doctrine of creation.

---

[34]Tertullianus, *Apol.*, 21 (*SVF* I, 533) and many other testimonies.
[35]*Retractationes*, I, 5, 3.
[36]*Retractationes*, I, 10, 4.
[37]*Epist.* 166, 2, 3. The doctrine criticized by Augustine is a central theme of Stoic thought. Since divinity is thought to be immanent in the cosmos, souls are particles of the divine Spirit animating the universe. This viewpoint already proclaimed by ancient Stoicism may also be found in the letters of Seneca: "Ratio autem nihil aliud est quam in corpus humanum pars divini spiritus mersa"(*Epist.* 66, 12; 120, 15; Hermias, *Irris. gent. phil.* 14 [*SVF* I, 495]).

On the one hand, he had to interpret the text from *Genesis*, according to which God performed his work of creation in six days and sanctified the seventh, as well as a passage from *Ecclesiasticus* (XVIII, 1), which states that God created all things at once. On the other hand, he could hardly deny that the world is constantly evolving and developing. New beings come to be and others pass away. Creation seemingly goes on without interruption. In order to reconcile the biblical teaching with daily experience, Augustine appeals to the Stoic theory of seminal reasons. Whatever happens in the world is not due to accident or to blind fate. God himself, by means of seminal reasons, determined the course according to which events will unfold during the flow of time.[38]

Augustine compares this to the growth of a tree. A seed already contains in invisible and hidden fashion whatever the further development of the tree will bring to light. One must be aware of the later evolution of the tree in order to grasp all of the possibilities present in the seed.[39] Augustine applies this comparison to the world's creation. Creation as it is described in *Genesis* is somewhat ambiguous. In a sense, creation was completed after six days, since the Creator had already produced the seeds for everything. What will follow is only the organic unfolding of a history whose components were already present in seminal fashion from the beginning. Consequently, we may say that from the beginning God produced the causes of all subsequent evolution. This, in turn, is only the organic and vital manifestation of possibilities already present from the beginning.[40] Hence, there is in the world a natural evolution, already established and fixed by the Creator to the extent that he is bound by the seminal reasons he has introduced into things. He can produce from these seminal reasons all the possibilities they contain; but he is unable to make them give rise to something he has excluded from their development.[41]

Man is also included in this seminal creation. The history of mankind as a whole, like the history of each individual, is encompassed within the initial creation, even though the soul of the first

---

[38] *De Gen. ad litt.*, IV, 33, 52.
[39] *De Gen. ad litt.*, II, 15, 30; V, 23, 45; VI, 16, 27.
[40] *De Gen. ad litt.*, VI, 11, 18.
[41] *De Gen. ad litt.*, IX, 17, 32.

man was directly created by God.⁴² The development of man's history is the organic growth of that which has already been created at the level of causes.⁴³

This doctrine does not mean, however, that everything was settled in the beginning. In Augustine's view there is always organic and vital development, within which real enrichment remains possible. The most delicate issue is that of human freedom. For Augustine man is definitely endowed with the ability to arrange the course of his life, even though this power was deeply wounded by original sin. As regards seminal reasons, Augustine wonders whether they are at the origin of a progressive evolution of beings, or whether they suddenly produce beings in completed state (in accord with the generally accepted view that the first man was directly created as a mature individual).⁴⁴

Augustine accepts both of these alternatives at the same time. If one admits of nothing but progressive development, one must face the problem of miracles, for instance, the sudden change of water into wine. On the other hand, if one allows for instantaneous transformations, one must account for the gradual evolution of nature attested to by daily experience. In Augustine's view, seminal reasons enable one to account for both ways of coming to be.⁴⁵

He applies this viewpoint to the creation of the first man. This was carried out in accord with the factors contained within the seminal reasons. If Adam was created as a mature individual, this was because that way of coming to be had been fixed by seminal reasons. It is possible, however, for some indetermination to remain in the constitution of these seminal reasons. In such cases, the manner of production will depend on God's will as this is expressed in the actual production.⁴⁶ Consequently, the creation of the world was produced and completed within the course of six days. This is to say that God introduced into the world seminal reasons which already contained in inchoative fashion the entire later evolution, with the exception of that which God has kept within the inner recesses of his own will. Even that which God has preserved in the hidden secrets

---

⁴²*De Gen. ad litt.*, VI, 11, 19. Cf. E. Portalié, "Augustin (Saint)," *Dict. de Théol. Cath.*, cols. 2353 and 2360.
⁴³*De Gen. ad litt.*, VI, 15, 26.
⁴⁴*De Gen. ad litt.*, VI, 14, 25.
⁴⁵*De Gen. ad litt.*, VI, 14, 25.
⁴⁶*De Gen. ad litt.*, VI, 15, 26.

of his providence should be in accord with the elements he has introduced into the seminal reasons.⁴⁷

The doctrine of seminal reasons comes from the Stoics. It was developed and elaborated within the materialistic framework of their philosophy. The same theory, however, was adopted by Plotinus and interpreted within his spiritualistic context. While Plotinus borrowed this teaching from the Stoics, he gave it a new meaning in light of his own thought.⁴⁸ Clearly, then, the doctrine of seminal reasons is not necessarily linked either to a materialistic or to a spiritualistic philosophy. In Augustine's case it is difficult to determine whether he borrowed this teaching directly from the Stoics or indirectly through the mediation of Plotinus. According to Augustine's own testimony, the influence of both Stoicism and Epicureanism was not strong at the end of the fourth century and the beginning of the fifth. These doctrines, he notes, were hardly treated in the schools of rhetoric. They already belonged to a bygone era.⁴⁹ This may be true insofar as explicit teaching is concerned; but Western thought, and even Christian doctrine, had already been deeply influenced by Stoic categories during the previous period.

During the fifth century the influence of Neoplatonism gradually became stronger. In the philosophical schools of Athens and Alexandria the general tendency was decidedly in favor of Neoplatonic thought. Many members of these schools wrote commentaries on Aristotle's works. They interpreted these in the sense of Neoplatonic spiritualism and tried to show, as a defense against the Christians, that there was no real opposition between Plato and Aristotle.

Nemesius of Emesa, a Christian bishop, firmly rejected Stoic materialism. According to him, the human soul cannot be corporeal, for then it could not be a principle of unity and order for the body. If the soul is corporeal, it too will need a unifying principle.⁵⁰

---

⁴⁷*De Gen. ad litt.*, VI, 18, 29.
⁴⁸*Enn.* II, 3, 12; II, 3, 13; II, 3, 14; II, 3, 15; II, 3, 16; III, 2, 2; IV, 3, 10; IV, 4, 11; IV, 4, 16; IV, 4, 29; V, 3, 8; V, 3, 9; V, 7, 3; V, 7, 5; V, 9, 6 and also some other passages.
⁴⁹*Epist.* 118, 3, 21: Quos jam certe nostra aetate sic obmutuisse conspicimus, ut vix jam in scholis rhetorum commemoretur tantum, quae fuerint illorum sententiae.
⁵⁰*De natura hominis*, ed. Verbeke and Moncho, II, pp. 24, 41–25, 50. According to H. Dörrie (*Porphyrios' "Symmikta Zetemata"*, Zetemata, Heft 20 [Münster, 1959], p. 130) this argument was borrowed from Porphyry.

As to the argument that the soul penetrates into the whole body and extends into the three dimensions, Nemesius replies that by itself the soul is unextended. It is extended only *per accidens* as a result of its union with the body.[51]

This argumentation also appears in the writings of Faustus of Riez, but his conclusion is quite different. According to him the soul must be quantitative and corporeal, because it is closely linked to the body. It is located within the body and extends throughout the various parts of the bodily organism.[52] Of course human thinking is not necessarily enclosed within the limits of the body. A man can think of objects that are far removed from him and which cannot be directly perceived. This does not imply, however, that human soul is present everywhere, or at least that it is not strictly located within the body. According to Faustus, even when soul is concerned with an object that does not fall within our immediate vicinity, it does not leave the body to which it is united. It is only at the moment of death that the soul abandons the body.[53] Since it resides within the limits of an extended body which it entirely permeates, soul should possess the same quantitative extension and be corporeal.

Does this psychological materialism also imply that the divine substance is corporeal? Definitely not, maintains Faustus. God is the only incorporeal being. Whatever other beings may exist as intermediary between man and God are corporeal.[54] The meaning of this teaching is clear. According to the Stoics, human soul is a particle of the divine substance, and present everywhere as an immanent animating principle. Neither Tertullian nor Lactantius accepted this kind of pan(en)theism. They always emphasized the

---

[51]*De natura hominis*, ed. Verbeke and Moncho, II, pp. 25, 63–26, 71; p. 26, 68: Essentialiter igitur et ipsi animae secundum se ipsam quidem non insunt tres dimensiones, secundum accidens vero eo quod est in eo quod habet tres dimensiones, conspicitur et ipsa habens tres dimensiones.

[52]*Epist*. 3, p. 175, 7 Engelbr. (C.S.E.L., t. 21): Quomodo non localis est, quae inserta membris et inligata visceribus solis motibus vaga conditione substantiae tenetur inclusa?; cf. *Epist*. 5, p. 188, 24: Deus non alicubi est: quod alicubi est continetur loco, quod continetur loco corpus est.

[53]*Epist*. 3, p. 177, 2 Engelbr.: Unde hoc magis ipsa conscientiis nostris ratio loquitur, quod unaquaeque anima aut multiplicia cogitare rerum causis intra se concepta parturiat aut sensus suos velut quaedam officia aut ministeria diversis necessitatibus occupanda dispergat, ipsa vero in conclavi corporis sui semel de eo exitura requiescat; *Epist*. 3, p. 174, 12.

[54]*Epist*. 3, p. 180, 23 Engelbr.: unus Deus incorporeus.

distinction between God and man, although they regarded both as corporeal. In stating that God is the only incorporeal being, Faustus adopted the same point of view. If human soul is corporeal, it cannot be a particle of an incorporeal substance. Faustus's teaching points mainly to the unique nature of the divine being. All creatures are corporeal; angels and human souls are corporeal. To be material is distinctive of whatever has been produced by the divine Creator.[55] At a time when Neoplatonism was becoming more and more influential, this view is easy enough to understand. It involves a criticism of the doctrine of emanation, according to which only one lower being flows from the first principle, with this lower being in its turn producing another one. Thus emanation continues onward, producing gradually lower and lower levels of perfection, down to the final one—matter. This doctrine does not clearly draw the distinction between God and created beings. All lower beings necessarily proceed from the highest principle. In a sense they belong to the very nature of that principle. Faustus's teaching is clearly at variance both with Stoic theology and with the Neoplatonic view of the principal hypostases.

It is clear that Faustus is not the only one to profess this theory. As E.L. Fortin has shown, it was also defended by Vincentius Victor,[56] by Cassianus, by Hilary of Poitiers, by Gennadius of Marseille, and by Arnobius Junior.[57] On the other hand, a spiritualistic psychology was espoused by Saint Augustine, Claudianus Mamertus, and Cassiodorus, as well as by Nemesius of Emesa, whose *De natura hominis* was twice translated into Latin during the Middle

---

[55]E.L. Fortin, *Christianisme et culture philosophique au cinquième siècle. La querelle de l'âme humaine en Occident* (Paris, 1959), pp. 51-52: "Cette conception s'était imposée avec une telle force que même un auteur comme Origène, tout en se prononçant nettement en faveur de l'existence des créatures spirituelles, n'osera pas soutenir qu'elles puissent se passer d'un élément matériel."

[56]Augustinus, *De anima et eius origine*, c. 419.

[57]E.L. Fortin, *Christianisme et culture philosophique*, p. 51, n. 5. The author refers to Cassianus, *Conlationes*, VII, 13, p. 193, 5 Petschenig (C.S.E.L., t. 13); Hilarius apud Claud. Mam., *De statu animae*, p. 135, 2 Engelbr. and some other passages; Gennadius, *Liber sive diffinitio ecclesiasticorum dogmatum*, 11, p. 91 Turner (*Journal of Theological Studies*, t. 7, 1106); 12, p. 92; Arnobius, *Conflictus cum Serapione*, II, 5, *PL* 53, col. 276; *Commentarii in psalmos*, ibid., col. 437 B. Cf. M. Spanneut, *Permanence du Stoïcisme*, pp. 148-50.

Ages. According to M. Spanneut, materialism had its representatives in the Latin West up until the seventh century. During the ninth century the nature of the soul was examined once more. The question was raised whether the human soul is corporeal, and from whence it comes. Discussion was also directed to another topic—whether all human souls form a unity, or whether they are independent principles. About 850 Charles the Bald addressed a questionnaire to the Cathedral School of Reims. The question raised immediately reminds one of fifth-century discussions concerning the nature of the soul. The problem was this— whether God must be regarded as the only being without any material basis, the only one that is totally incorporeal.[58] In his *De animae ratione*, Alcuin, taking his inspiration from St. Augustine, upholds the incorporeal nature of the soul, though he acknowledges that it is difficult to determine its true being.[59] According to him, human soul is an intellectual and rational *spiritus*, capable of both good and evil, endowed with freedom, invisible and incorporeal, and totally present in each of the bodily members.[60] The soul governs the body by means of the most subtle material elements, light and air.[61] As to the origin of souls, the author believes it impossible for man to discover this. Only God knows this.[62] Hrabanus Maurus also adopted a spiritualistic viewpoint in his *De anima*, which was written at the request of Lotharius I, and wherein he is influenced by Cassiodorus.[63] Another question about the soul had also been raised by King Charles: *Sitne anima circumscripta sive localis*? (Is the soul confined within the bounds of a limited space?) This question was answered by Ratramnus.

[58] A.H. Armstrong, *The Cambridge History of Later Greek and Early Medieval Philosophy* (Cambridge, 1967), p. 574.
[59] Alcuinus, *De animae ratione liber*, PL 101, 639–50; cf. 639: animae vero rationem vix paucorum est pleniter nosse.
[60] Alcuinus, *De animae ratione*, 643: anima seu animus est spiritus intellectualis rationalis, semper in motu, semper vivens, bonae malaeque voluntatis capax; secundum benignitatem Creatoris libero arbitrio nobilitatus, sua voluntate vitiatus.
[61] Alcuinus, *De animae ratione*, 644: Quae etiam per lucem et aerem, quae sunt excellentiora mundi corpora, corpus administrat suum. This doctrine was adopted by several philosophers. It stems from Neoplatonism, but it is also connected with Stoic psychology.
[62] Alcuinus, *De animae ratione*, 645.
[63] Ph. Delhaye, *Une controverse sur l'âme universelle au IXe siècle* (Louvain, 1950), p. 19.

If most of the authors dealing with the nature of the soul defend its spiritual character, at least one of them proposes a different answer. This is Paulus Alvarus of Cordoba. He is mainly concerned with the origin of the human soul. In relying on St. Jerome, he mentions five different positions concerning this. Some believe that souls proceed from heaven (Pythagoreans, Platonists, Origen). Others maintain that they stem from the divine substance (Stoics, Manichaeans, representatives of the Priscillian heresy). Still others teach that they were created some time ago and that they have been preserved as a kind of treasure. Then there are the representatives of traducianism: Tertullian, Apollinarius, and the great majority of Western thinkers (*maxima pars occidentalium*). Finally, the author refers to Jerome's view, that souls are created every day.[64] Paulus flatly rejects Jerome's doctrine, which had already been opposed by Augustine. According to Paulus, it is impossible to admit that children dying without baptism are punished if their souls have been directly created by God.[65] That view is compatible only with traducianism, an important Stoic theory.

If we may rely on Paulus Alvarus, in the ninth century the great majority of Western thinkers favored traducianism, a materialistic Stoic doctrine. According to Odo of Cambrai, traducianism was still widely accepted in the twelfth century. He explicitly states that many believe that the procreation of souls is like that of bodies. Souls, too, arise from insemination.[66] Given this background, one is not surprised to find that William of Saint-Thierry strongly attacks the teaching of "some crazy philosophers" (*stultorum quorumdam philosophorum*) who are materialists in the full sense of that term. They maintain that whatever exists is corporeal. Even God would be a combination of material elements, for he coincides with the harmony of nature. According to them, the soul must be viewed in the same way.[67] On the strength of this testimony, it is difficult to say

---

[64]Paulus Alvarus Cordubensis, *Epist.* V, *PL* 121, 453: St. Jerome teaches about the souls: quotidie a Deo creantur.

[65]Paulus Alvarus, *Epist.* V, 457.

[66]Odo of Cambrai, *De peccato originali*, II; *PL* 160, 1077: Sunt tamen multi qui volunt animam ex traduce fieri sicut corpus et cum corporis semine vim etiam animae procedere.

[67]Guilelmus of Saint-Thierry, *De erroribus, PL* 180, 340: Stultorum quorundam philosophorum videtur sententiam sequi, dicentium nihil prorsus esse praeter corpora et corporea: non aliud esse Deus in mundo quam

what kind of materialism William has in mind. Alan of Lille also attacks some contemporary materialists who hold that the human spirit (*spiritus*) disappears when an individual dies, and that resurrection is impossible. The term *spiritus* probably refers to Stoic terminology. In the twelfth century the origin and nature of the soul continued to be debated. The presence of Stoicism in this controversy can hardly be denied.

A second topic that was seriously debated in the ninth century had to do with unity versus multiplicity of souls. Is there only one universal soul, or a multiplicity of individual souls?[68] This problem had already been raised by Augustine in his *De quantitate animae*. There he wonders whether there is only one soul, or simultaneously one and many souls, or perhaps a multiplicity of independent souls. What lies behind this problem? According to the Stoics there is at once world-soul, which coincides with the divine substance, and many individual souls. These are thought to be particles of the immanent Reason. According to Plotinus, universal soul is one of the three principal hypostases, the third, from which all individual souls proceed. Augustine could hardly admit that there is only one soul. This would be incompatible with individual existence and freedom. He also rejects the doctrine of a multiplicity of independent souls, since all individual souls must come from the same higher principle. As to the proper nature of this relationship, Augustine was unable to offer a satisfactory solution: do individual souls directly depend upon the divine Creator, or only through the intermediary of a universal soul?[69]

During the ninth century the question arises again in a discussion between Ratramnus of Corbie and a monk from the diocese of Beauvais. This monk adopts the view of Macarius Scotus and defends the existence of a universal soul from which individual souls proceed.[70] The existence of a common soul as a substantial reality is also admitted by Odo of Cambrai.[71] In his reply Ratramnus inter-

---

concursum elementorum et temperaturam naturae; et hoc ipsum esse animam in corpore.

[68]Cf. Ph. Delhaye, *Une controverse sur l'âme universelle au IXe siècle*; I only want to deal with this controversy insofar as it is related to the subject of my study.

[69]*De quantitate animae*, 32, 69.

[70]Ph. Delhaye, *Une controverse sur l'âme universelle au IXe siècle*, p. 20.

[71]Ph. Delhaye, *Une controverse sur l'âme universelle au IXe siècle*, p. 20;

prets Augustine's question in a logical way—is there a universal concept of soul? According to Ratramnus, the notion (*species*) of soul is both one and many, not simultaneously, however, but according to different usages.[72] Ratramnus firmly rejects Stoic materialism and traducianism,[73] as well as the existence of a subsistent nature, characterized by its own qualities, from which individual souls would proceed. In his eyes such a doctrine is incompatible with Christian faith and, for that matter, does not even agree with the teaching of pagan philosophers.[74] He finally concludes that each individual possesses his own soul.[75]

This question was again raised during the twelfth century. In a work entitled *De mundi constitutione* (dating from the twelfth century) we read that there is only one soul, the world-soul. This provides every being with its appropriate capacities and powers.[76] According to William of Conches the expression *anima mundi* may be taken in three different ways. Some identify the world-soul with the Holy Spirit. This was the view of Thierry of Chartres and of William himself during the first stage of his development. According to a second interpretation, the world-soul is a natural power introduced by God into sensible reality. This corresponds to the position of Alan of Lille, who identifies nature with the world-soul. It may have also been the view of Bernardus Silvestris, according to whom there is an affinity between the substance of the world-soul and that of the heavenly bodies and of air.[77] This position clearly reveals

---

cf. *De peccato originali*, lib. 2 (*PL* 160, 1079).

[72]Ph. Delhaye, *Une controverse sur l'âme universelle au IXe siècle*, p. 25; pp. 40–43.

[73]Ratramnus of Corbie, *Liber de anima ad Odonem Bellovacensem*, ed. D.C. Lambot, Analecta Mediaevalia Namurcensia, 2 (Namur-Lille, 1951), p. 131: Corporalem autem dici animam non est catholicum. Catholica namque testatur ecclesia animas humanas incorporeas esse, et ad similitudinem dei conditas.

[74]Ratramnus, *Liber de anima*, p. 135: Videtur itaque introduci naturam quamdam subsistentem, suisque qualitatibus subiectam, de qua fiat animarum procreatio. Quod non est christianum, verum etiam nec philosophorum gentilium.

[75]Ratramnus, *Liber de anima*, p. 140.

[76]*De mundi constitutione*, *PL* 90, 902–3: Dicunt etiam quidam unam tantum esse animam, idest mundanam.

[77]T. Gregory, *Anima mundi. La filosofia di Guglielmo di Conches e la scuola di Chartres* (Florence, no date), p. 181.

The Challenge of Materialism 39

Stoic influences and is probably related to Seneca and Virgil. According to E. Gilson, however, Bernardus combined both the second interpretation and the third. The third position holds that world-soul is an incorporeal substance which is present in all corporeal beings.[78] William of Conches eventually abandoned his first position. If the world-soul was created, it cannot be identified with the Holy Spirit.[79] At the end of his career William probably gave up the entire position concerning world-soul, even as it had already been abandoned in the tenth century by Bavo of Corvey. In treating of Boethius's *anima mundi* Bavo had commented that it was a specifically philosophical theory, and far removed from Christian belief.[80]

The most extreme kind of materialism and monism are to be found in the *Quaternuli* of David of Dinant. Whatever the direct influences on David may have been, monism and materialism are characteristic features of Stoicism. In addition, David refers to Zeno, the founder of the Stoic School.[81]

When dealing with the composition of man, Thomas Aquinas always maintains that the human soul is incorporeal but he repeatedly asks whether there is an intermediary between body and soul, some kind of link between these two components which differ in nature, one being material and the other immaterial. In this context Thomas refers to the teaching of some Platonists (*quidam Platonici*) who hold that the two constituents of man are joined by a corporeal link. Some think that this intermediary is an incorruptible body which is never separated from the intellective soul.[82] Others hold

---

[78]É. Gilson, "La cosmogonie de Bernardus Sylvestris," *Arch. doctr. litt. du M.A.* (1928), p. 16.
[79]T. Gregory, *Anima mundi*, pp. 113ff.
[80]A.H. Armstrong, *Later Greek and Early Medieval Philosophy*, p. 589.
[81]*Davidis de Dinanto Quaternulorum fragmenta*, ed. Marianus Kurdzialek, Studia Mediewisticzne, 3 (Warsaw, 1963), pp. 70-71: Ex hiis ergo colligi potest mentem et ylen idem esse . . . Manifestum est igitur unam solam substanciam esse, non tantum omnium corporum, sed etiam animarum omnium et eam nichil aliud esse, quam ipsum Deum. In this context David mentions the names of Plato, Zeno and Socrates: Si ergo mundus est ipse Deus preter se ipsum perceptibile sensui, ut Plato et Zeno et Socrates et multi alii dixerunt, yle igitur mundi est ipse Deus. The Zeno mentioned in this passage must be the founder of the Stoic School. He maintained that the world and God coincide and that both are corporeal.
[82]*Summa Theologiae*, I, q. 76, a. 7 in c.: Quorum quidam Platonici

that it is a kind of material spirit or a luminous body, similar to the fifth element of the heavenly spheres.[83]

Aquinas categorically rejects any such position. The soul is the substantial form of a material principle and cannot be joined to the body by means of any corporeal link. Thomas does admit, however, that the soul moves the bodily organs with the help of a material spirit. This spirit is the first instrument of the power of motion.[84]

Aquinas's immediate sources for information concerning this psychological position are evident. One is Augustine, who states that the soul governs the body by means of a subtle nature—light and air.[85] Another is the *De spiritu et anima* which is attributed to Alcher of Clairvaux.[86] Finally there is the *De differentia spiritus et animae* of Costa ben Luca (864–923). It can hardly be doubted that this doctrine comes from Neoplatonism. It can be found in Plotinus,

---

dixerunt quod anima intellectiva habet corpus incorruptibile sibi naturaliter unitum, a quo numquam separatur, et eo mediante unitur corpori hominis corruptibili. According to this Neoplatonic doctrine even the intellective soul, although it is immaterial, could not exist without being joined to something corporeal. Cf. Jean Philopon, *Commentaire sur le De anima d'Aristote, Traduction de Guillaume de Moerbeke. Édition critique avec une Introduction sur la psychologie de Philopon*, by G. Verbeke (Louvain, 1966), pp. xxxiii–xxxiv.

[83]*Summa Theologiae*, I, q. 76, a. 7 in c.: Quidam vero dixerunt quod unitur corpori mediante spiritu corporeo. Alii vero dixerunt quod unitur corpori mediante luce, quam dicunt esse corpus, et de natura quintae essentiae.

[84]*Summa Theologiae*, I, q. 76, a. 7, ad 1: Et primum instrumentum virtutis motivae est spiritus, ut dicit Philosophus in libro *de Causa motus animalium*; cf. *De motu animalium*, 10, 703a19-22; G. Verbeke, "Doctrine du pneuma et entéléchisme chez Aristote," in *Aristotle on Mind and the Senses*, ed. G.E.R. Lloyd and G.E.L. Owen (Cambridge, 1978), pp. 196-97.

[85]*De Gen. ad litt.*, VII, 15, 21: Quapropter non est quidem humanae animae natura nec de terra nec de aqua nec de aere nec de igne quolibet: sed tamen crassioris corporis sui materiam hoc est humidam quamdam terram, quae in carnis versa est qualitatem, per subtilioris naturam corporis, administrat, idest per lucem et aerem.

[86]Aquinas mentions already·that this treatise had been falsely attributed to St. Augustine (*Qu. de Anima*, a. 9, ad 1). In this work one of the meanings of the term *spiritus* is described in this way: Spiritus etiam est quaedam vis animae, mente inferior, ubi corporalium rerum similitudines exprimuntur. Cf. L. Norpoth, *Der pseudo-augustinische Traktat: De spiritu et anima* [Doctoral dissertation, Munich, 1924] (Cologne-Bochum, 1971), pp. 99-106.

Porphyry, Iamblichus, Hierocles, and Proclus.[87] But there is still another source for this theory—Stoicism. According to the Stoics, human soul, as a particle of the Divine Reason, is a material spirit. The substance of the soul is *pneuma*, which means either a kind of fire that is beyond the four elements and gives origin to them, or a combination of air and fire.[88] Marcus Aurelius used a diminutive of *pneuma* (*pneumation*) to designate the link between body and mind. The Neoplatonists always emphasized the immaterial character of the soul; but instead of rejecting the Stoic *pneuma* they offered a new interpretation of it in accord with their own system. *Pneuma* or spirit became an intermediary between body and soul. Given this, both Neoplatonism and Stoicism provide the remote background for the question raised by Aquinas concerning the union of body and soul. As in so many other cases, here again Neoplatonism is dependent on Stoic teaching.[89]

Apparently during the second half of the thirteenth century materialism continued to be a critical point. Among the theses condemned by the Bishop of Paris in 1270, at least two refer to materialistic positions. Treating of philosophical anthropology, one of the condemned propositions states that the soul, being the formal principle of man, passes away when the body is corrupted.[90] Presumably the immediate background for this teaching is the Aristotelian view that the soul is the first actuality (entelechy) of a bodily organism that possesses life potentially. At the beginning of his *De anima* Aristotle wonders whether the human soul can exist independently from the body. In his view, the answer depends upon the reply to another question—whether any human activity is totally independent from the body.[91] Aristotle's answer to this second ques-

---

[87]Cf. G. Verbeke, *L'évolution de la doctrine du pneuma*, pp. 384–85: "D'une façon générale, le pneuma constitue le lien entre les êtres immatériels et le monde matériel. En psychologie, le corps lumineux se présente comme une auréole entourant l'âme et la préservant du contact dégradant de l'organisme matériel qu'elle anime."
[88]Cf. G. Verbeke, *L'évolution de la doctrine du pneuma*, p. 173.
[89]Cf. G. Verbeke, *L'évolution de la doctrine du pneuma*, p. 171.
[90]The proposition is formulated in the following way: Quod anima que est forma hominis secundum quod homo, corrumpitur, corrupto corpore.
[91]*De Anima*, I, 1, 403a3ff. In Aristotle's view the soul is the principle and source of human activity. By analyzing the character of this activity, one is able to discover the nature of the psychic principle. Every principle acts

tion must be negative. Not even man's highest activity, thinking, is totally independent from the body, since it relies on sense perception. As a consequence, Aristotle was forced to reject life after death for the soul.[92]

Another proposition condemned by the Bishop of Paris concerns human freedom. The condemned proposition states that everything occurring on earth is necessitated by heavenly bodies.[93] Relying on the testimony of Boethius, Aquinas refers this teaching back to the Stoics and connects it with their theory of knowledge.[94] The Stoics maintain that all human knowledge, including intellection, results from action exercised on the soul by corporeal things. These things impress their copy on the soul like images in a mirror or letters on a white paper. This means that our psychic principle receives impressions from without in passive fashion, without exercising any activity of its own.[95] In such a theory, heavenly bodies play an important role. Our intellectual knowledge stems mainly from these higher beings. And because the human soul is purely passive with respect to heavenly bodies in acquiring intellectual knowledge, it is totally necessitated by them in its activities. Hence free decisions and freely initiated acts are eliminated.[96]

---

according to its nature. Hence all activity is a constant disclosure of its cause.

[92]Cf. G. Verbeke, "Comment Aristote conçoit-il l'immatériel?" *Revue philos. de Louvain* 44 (1946), pp. 205–36. Pietro Pomponazzi, in his *Tractatus de immortalitate animae*, ed. Gianfranco Morra (Bologna, 1954), deals with the same question and offers a reply that is more sophisticated. According to him the question of the immortality of the soul is a "neutrum problema." Neither the immortality nor the mortality of the soul can be proved. There are no decisive arguments supporting either of the alternatives. In this respect the author mentions Aquinas: Quare nolui ponere responsiones ad alteram partem, cum alii ponant, et praecipue Divus Thomas luculenter, copiose et graviter. Quapropter dicemus, sicut dixit Plato in prima *De legibus* certificare de aliquo, cum multi ambigunt, solius est Dei (*op. cit.*, p. 232).

[93]Quod omnia que hic in inferioribus aguntur, subsunt necessitati corporum celestium.

[94]*Summa contra Gentiles*, III, 85, n. 2614, ed. C. Pera: Per haec autem excluditur positio Stoicorum, qui ponebant omnes actus nostros, et etiam electiones nostras, secundum corpora caelestia disponi.

[95]*Summa contra Gentiles*, III, 84, n. 2592, ed. C. Pera.

[96]*Summa contra Gentiles*, III, 84, n. 2592, ed. C. Pera: Secundum quorum (scil. Stoicorum) sententiam sequebatur quod maxime ex impressione

The Challenge of Materialism 43

This summary does not entirely square with authentic Stoic teaching. The Stoics hold that human soul is a spark of the divine Spirit that governs the world and all that occurs in it. Man is unable to change the course of events because this is constantly determined by Divine Reason. Human freedom, however, is not denied. On the contrary, it is emphasized, but it is confined to man's internal attitude. It depends upon each individual whether he behaves in conformity with divine Logos or not; but whatever he does cannot influence in any way the course of history.[97] The Stoics defend the possibility of divination. It is possible for one to predict the future by observing the heavenly bodies. The entire cosmos forms an organic whole. Every part of the world is linked to every other part. In other words, there is a universal sympathy.

Aquinas's reaction to the Stoic position is quite negative. Intellectual knowledge is not purely passive. Man's intellect forms propositions, shapes arguments, and grasps universals and immaterial forms. His intellectual knowledge is not confined to images of the material world, but displays an activity that goes beyond corporeal reality.[98] The heavenly bodies are corporeal beings. They could never necessitate the human soul, which is incorporeal. Aquinas's position does not imply that the will's activity is merely spiritual or immaterial. Like that of the mind, its activity is linked to the body, to sense experience, and to appetitive life; but it is not performed by means of any corporeal instrument. It is not subjectively dependent

---

corporum caelestium intellectuales notiones nobis imprimerentur. Unde et Stoici fuerunt qui praecipue necessitate quadam fatali hominum vitam duci posuerunt.
  [97]Cf. G. Verbeke, "Aristotélisme et Stoïcisme dans le *De Fato* d'Alexandre d'Aphrodisias," *Arch. f. Gesch. d. Philos.* 50 (1968), pp. 91–92. The Stoics certainly accept universal determinism, because nothing in the universe could happen without having a cause: "Il y a donc une concaténation infrangible de causes et d'effets, d'antécédents et de conséquents; c'est rompre l'unité du cosmos que d'introduire une κίνησις ἀναίτιος." And yet Stoicism is also a philosophy of internal liberation from any power opposing the development of man according to his true rational nature. Both aspects are constantly present in Stoic teaching, although it is difficult to reconcile them with one another.
  [98]*Summa contra Gentiles*, III, 84, n. 2592, ed. C. Pera: Et sic manifestum est quod intellectus non est sicut recipiens imagines corporum, sed habet aliquam virtutem corporibus altiorem.

upon the bodily organism.[99] Thus Aquinas rejects this kind of determinism because of its materialism.

* * *

Stoic materialism was introduced into Christian thought almost from the beginning of our era. Tertullian and Lactantius were the main representatives of early Christian materialism. At one point in his intellectual development even Augustine sympathized with these views. Later on, in the fifth century, universal materialism was mitigated, presumably owing to the impact of Neoplatonism. Many Christian writers maintained that God is the only incorporeal being. In this form, materialism was frequently discussed from the ninth to the twelfth centuries. Many Christians were inclined to accept Stoic traducianism as a way of accounting for the transmission of original sin. Also, the doctrine of world-soul, taken in a materialistic way, was accepted by some important twelfth-century writers. In the thirteenth century, too, Stoic materialism was not entirely absent. Without being accepted, it was carefully examined and discussed, especially with reference to the nature and activity of the human soul and the question of human freedom. Hence, one may conclude that Stoic materialism was present from the early Christian period throughout the Middle Ages. It served as a kind of challenge, an issue that was constantly discussed, a question for which there was no uniform answer.

[99]The position of Aquinas in this respect is rather qualified. He does not declare that all influence of heavenly bodies on human behavior should be rejected. He only excludes a *direct* impact of celestial bodies on our decisions, without denying the possibility of an indirect influence: Sciendum est tamen quod, licet corpora caelestia directe intelligentiae nostrae causae esse non possint, aliquid tamen ad hoc operantur indirecte (*Summa contra Gentiles*, III, 84, n. 2596, ed. C. Pera).

CHAPTER III

ETHICAL PERSPECTIVES

The Stoics introduced a new pattern of moral life into the history of human thinking. This pattern was extremely influential and even contributed in shaping the moral ideals of Christianity. During the Middle Ages Stoic ethical perspectives were constantly present, even as they had been in patristic literature.[1] According to the Stoics, man should live in harmony with nature. This means that man should behave virtuously, since nature drives each individual to act in conformity with the norms of virtue. Nature is not an irrational impulse. It coincides with universal reason, which itself is present in whatever exists and which brings to pass the evolution of the world. This creative reason is nothing but immanent Divinity which represents the supreme law of moral life.

According to Stoic philosophy, man's basic moral fault consists in rejecting and internally opposing the course of history—the temporal manifestation of the divine Principle. In this context the area of moral activity is rather limited. Essentially it consists in accepting internally the course of events as they happen to occur. Man is unable to introduce any change into them. He may adopt a rebellious attitude, but this will be ineffective. The course of history goes on irresistibly. Man may accept the development of events, but this acceptance matters only for him, for his own conscience. It does not change the physiognomy of the world.[2]

---

[1]Cf. M. Spanneut, *Le Stoïcisme des Pères de l'Eglise de Clément de Rome à Clément d'Alexandrie*, 2nd ed. (Paris, 1969).

[2]Cf. A. Jagu, *Zénon de Cittium. Son rôle dans l'établissement de la morale stoïcienne* (Paris, 1946), pp. 18–19: "Mais alors qu'Aristote et les philosophes antérieurs ne désignaient par 'nature' que la nature individuelle, Zénon, au contraire, entend par là à la fois la nature universelle et la nature individuelle qui n'en est qu'un fragment." According to Diogenes Laërtios some disagreement about the meaning of nature existed between Cleanthes and Chrysippus. Whereas the first interpreted this term as referring only to common nature, the latter understood it as signifying both common and individual nature. Cleanthes actually insists on the permanent

In his *De legibus* Cicero adopts this Stoic viewpoint. There is a supreme law which dominates all moral conduct. This is natural law (*naturam sequi et eius quasi lege vivere*).[3] Natural law was not invented by man. It is an eternal wisdom that governs the world and dictates what should be done and what avoided. This wisdom coincides with the divine intellect. It is a rational principle which constantly inclines us to act morally. Such a law need not be written. Man does not have to learn it, since it is inborn in every human being (*diffusa in omnes*). It can never be abrogated. Neither the Senate nor the people can ever dispense from its prescriptions. This law is the same in Rome, in Athens, and everywhere else. It is the same for all times, for it is planned, elaborated, and promulgated by the divine Ruler.[4] Every positive law is ultimately grounded on this more fundamental norm, natural law. Within this perspective positive legislation is a symptom of moral decline. According to Seneca, written laws were unknown to primitive civilization. Only later, when vice gradually crept into human behavior, were laws invented and imposed.[5] In his *Pro Milone* Cicero speaks of a law that is unwritten and inborn. No one has to learn it, because it belongs to the natural structure of each individual. We know it because we participate in universal reason.[6]

According to the Stoics, law and legal prescriptions are not autonomous creations of the human mind which would determine on its own authority what is to be done or avoided. The very essence of human reason participates in the universal law that governs the world's development. Human mind transcends the narrow frontiers of any individual human existence. It places each existence within the organic order of the entire universe. Legal and moral rules are not a kind of compulsion that is imposed from without. On the contrary, they correspond to the basic dynamism of our being and are expressed in intuitions of our mind. Nor does the juridical and moral order result from arbitrary human agreement. It is prior to any convention because it belongs to man's metaphysical condition

---

danger of conflict between universal divine law and individual conduct (G. Verbeke, *Kleanthes van Assos* [Brussels, 1949], pp. 202-3).

[3] *De legibus*, I, 21, 56; II, 4, 8; II, 4, 10.
[4] *De republica*, III, 22, 33.
[5] Seneca, *Epist.* 90, 6.
[6] *Pro Milone*, 10.

and to the makeup of the universe. Universal reason is expressed in laws through the intermediary of the human mind, which elaborates this natural order and invests it with a legal structure. All particular laws are ultimately related to immanent cosmic reason.[7] In support of this view Cicero appeals to the feeling of guilt that arises in man when he does something wrong. Man avoids wrongdoing not so much because he fears punishment but because it is contrary to the most intimate tendency of his rational nature.[8]

On the other hand, a legal rule may be unjust. Laws promulgated by tyrants cannot be regarded as just even if all citizens agree on them.[9] Hence it becomes possible for one to formulate a moral appreciation of legal prescriptions.[10] The question arises, however, whether man can know what is in conformity with nature. With respect to this Cicero refers to certain fundamental intuitions which are present in all human beings—a natural and spontaneous consciousness of right and wrong. He speaks of inchoative notions which are equally present in all men.[11] This corresponds to the Stoic doctrine of anticipations (προλήψεις) which are part of the natural cognitive patrimony of all individuals.[12] Some common notions (*communes notitiae*) are especially important because everyone knows and accepts them.[13] Every man possesses an anticipative knowledge of natural law, or right and wrong, a knowledge which in the course of life will be developed owing to a growing consciousness of what is appropriate for human beings (οἰκείωσις). This Stoic doctrine is diametrically opposed to the legal positivism of Epicurus and Carneades, who maintain that nothing is right by nature (*nihil justum esse natura*).[14]

It is not so easy to determine precisely the impact of Stoic ethics

---

[7]*De legibus*, I, 12, 33.
[8]*De legibus*, I, 14, 40–41.
[9]*De legibus*, I, 15, 42.
[10]*De legibus*, I, 16, 44.
[11]*De legibus*, I, 10, 30: the author mentions some "inchoatae intelligentiae." These notions are not fully developed or adequately specified. Cicero stresses the fact that they are equally present in all individuals (similiter in omnibus imprimuntur).
[12]*Aëtii Plac.*, IV, 11 (*SVF* II, 83).
[13]Seneca, *Epist.* 117, 6: He declares that the Stoics attach special value to anticipative knowledge (presumptions) existing in all men. For them universal agreement is a criterion of truth.
[14]Seneca, *Epist.* 97, 13.

on medieval thought, although we do know that it was very strong. The main difficulty results from the fact that Stoic moral principles were incorporated into Christian teaching at an early date. They were assimilated by Christian writers almost from the beginning of our era. In studying the notion of magnanimity, R.-A. Gauthier comments that Clement of Alexandria unhesitatingly adopted the entire Stoic moral vocabulary, and especially its terminology concerning virtues.[15] It has already been shown that authors such as Evagrius Ponticus were deeply influenced by Stoic teaching. For instance, the notion of *apatheia* (impassibility) plays an important part in his spiritual doctrine.[16] In the Latin West St. Ambrose, in his *De officiis*, presents an amalgamation of Stoic ethics and Christian moral teaching. Ambrose follows rather faithfully the corresponding work by Cicero, but the spirit that permeates his treatise is genuinely Christian. According to the Stoics man's only good is virtue. This represents the final end and happiness of human life. According to St. Ambrose the true goal for every human being is eternal life in God. Ambrose's treatise was very popular and exercised considerable influence during the Middle Ages.[16bis] Since Stoicism's influence on the Church Fathers has already been carefully studied, I shall here concentrate on a later period.

In the twelfth century several authors introduced some Stoic moral teaching into the Western world. William of Conches, in his *Moralium Dogma Philosophorum*, relies in the main on the writings of Cicero and Seneca. He refers to Seneca as the most elegant teacher of morality.[17] As has already been mentioned, this work was probably composed for Prince Henry, the future King Henry II of England. It is hardly original, since seven-eighths of the whole has

---

[15]R.-A. Gauthier, *Magnanimité, L'idéal de la grandeur dans la philosophie païenne et dans la théologie chrétienne* (Paris, 1951), p. 220.

[16]M. Spanneut, *Permanence du Stoïcisme*, p. 173. The Stoic notion of impassibility was adopted also, with more or less emphasis, by Clement of Alexandria, Origen, Basil the Great, Gregory of Nazianzus, Gregory of Nyssa and John Chrysostom.

[16bis]Th. Schmidt, *Ambrosius. Sein Werk De officiis libri tres und die Stoa* (Erlangen, 1897); Th. Deman, "Le 'De officiis' de S. Ambroise dans l'histoire de la théologie morale," *Rev. des sciences philos. et théol.* 37 (1953), pp. 409-24.

[17]J. Holmberg, *Das Moralium dogma philosophorum des Guillaume de Conches* (Uppsala, 1929).

been borrowed from other writings.[18] It includes 181 quotations from Cicero, primarily from the *De officiis* (165 quotations). Many other texts are borrowed from Seneca and from the *De remediis fortuitorum*. The main inspiration for this work is clearly Stoic. Reason is viewed as the basic norm for human conduct. Man should never depart from reason, not even in the most disturbing situations.[19] A moral man must be aware of the fact that only virtue is of value. Everything else is without real worth.[20] Whereas foolish people place the fruit of their conduct in honor and fame, the wise man puts it in his own conscience.[21] The reward for ethical behavior should not be sought in anything external, but in peace of conscience.[22] This corresponds with one of the characteristic Stoic teachings. Fame and honor do not have any real value. They belong to the category of the indifferent. Moreover, it is not man's duty to transform the external world in which he lives. The world does not need to be improved, and man is unable to introduce any change into the course of events as it has been established by the immanent Divinity. What matters for man is his internal attitude.

William also notes that by nature there is no private property. Private property springs either from ancient occupation (when people occupied territories which did not belong to any particular individual), or from victory in war (when the victor took possession of conquered lands), or from legal rules (when children by will receive an inheritance from their parents). William does not, however, advocate a return to common property. Everybody may retain what happens to be in his possession.[23]

As regards the notion of virtue, he views it as a steady disposition

---

[18]According to Ph. Delhaye it is highly probable that William of Conches is the author of the *Moralium dogma philosophorum*. Some controversy has arisen about this question (cf. Ph. Delhaye, "Une adaptation du *De officiis* au XIIe siècle. Le *Moralium dogma philosophorum*," *Recherches de théologie ancienne et médiévale* XVI [1949], pp. 227–58; XVII [1950], pp. 5–28; *Gauthier de Châtillon est-il l'auteur du Moralium dogma?* [Namur-Lille, 1953]).

[19]*Moralium dogma*, p. 36, 15: Fortis enim et constantis animi est non perturbari in rebus adversis, nec tumultuantem de gradu dehici, sed praesente consilio uti, nec a ratione discedere.

[20]*Moralium dogma*, p. 72, 1.
[21]*Moralium dogma*, p. 31, 16.
[22]*Moralium dogma*, p. 72, 23.
[23]*Moralium dogma*, p. 13, 3.

of the mind which corresponds to nature and is in agreement with reason. Every element of this definition seems to be inspired by Stoic ethics.[24] Within the hierarchy of virtues, William assigns the highest rank to temperance. It is owing to this moral attitude that man can govern himself. Fortitude and justice are directed to the government of family and city. According to William, it is of greater value to man for him to master himself than to dominate what is outside him. The fourth and lowest rank is assigned to prudence.[25] Decidedly Stoic influences predominate in this work. When one bears in mind that it was written for the education of a Christian prince, a future king of England, one realizes how important was this penetration of Stoic ethics in the twelfth-century renaissance.

Within the framework of Stoic ethics the virtue of magnanimity holds an important place. According to Chrysippus it is the wisdom that lifts us above the events of life, above whatever may happen in the lives of virtuous or immoral people. According to Chrysippus magnanimity is a subordinate virtue which flows from wisdom through the intermediary of the primary virtues. Panaetius, however, regards it as a primary virtue from which other moral dispositions proceed. In later Stoicism, courage, perseverance, and magnanimity are linked together and placed on the same level. They form a coherent triad.[26] The Stoic notion of magnanimity was introduced into the twelfth century mainly through Cicero and Seneca.[27] In his study of this subject, Gauthier mentions different authors who were influenced by Stoic teaching on this matter. These

---

[24]*Moralium dogma*, p. 7, 11: Virtus vero est habitus animi in modum nature rationi consentaneus.

[25]*Moralium dogma*, pp. 52ff.; p. 53, 8: Temperancia enim regit homo se ipsum, fortitudine et iusticia familiam et civitatem. Sed melius est homini dominium sui quam externum.

[26]R.-A. Gauthier, *Magnanimité*, pp. 150–64. The author summarizes the doctrine of Chrysippus as follows: "Les quatre vertus premières découlent donc *immédiatement* de la sagesse; mais toutes les autres vertus—et c'est ici que nous saisissons le sens de la doctrine des vertus subordonnées—toutes les autres vertus découlent immédiatement des vertus premières, et ne découlent de la sagesse que *médiatement*, par l'intermédiaire des vertus premières."

[27]According to R.-A. Gauthier (*Magnanimité*, p. 240) it was mainly through the *Formula vitae honestae* or *De quattuor virtutibus* that already in the twelfth century the idea of magnanimity was widely diffused among the people.

include Peter Cantor, Alan of Lille, William of Auvergne, and Bonaventure. The concept, however, was gradually transformed under the influence of Christianity, so much so that it completely lost its original meaning. Instead of being the embodiment of Stoic contempt for the world, magnanimity came to be identified with Christian humility.[28]

Peter Abelard's major ethical writing is entitled *Scito teipsum* (*Know Thyself*). This title points to the internal nature of moral behavior.[29] In Abelard's view, what matters from an ethical standpoint is not the external act, nor the emotional movements that may lead one to perform certain acts, but only the consent (*consensus*) of the individual who acts.[30] Moral fault or sin, when reduced to its essential nature, is always consent to evil recognized as such. Only consent may properly be called sin.[31] In developing this important notion, Abelard points to the fact that God takes into account the dispositions of the heart rather than the external act that is performed.[32] The external act cannot increase in the slightest degree the merit of the acting subject. The same is true of sinful behavior. Performance of the act does not increase moral fault, which resides totally in consent. The human soul can only be defiled by something that belongs to it, not by something external. In Abelard's view, the only element that really belongs to the soul is consent. This corresponds to the Stoic συγκατάθεσις; consent means that the individual freely and independently agrees upon a particular attitude.[33] Per-

---

[28]R.-A. Gauthier, *Magnanimité*, pp. 239-50. With respect to Bonaventure Gauthier writes: "Mais nous pourrons bientôt constater un phénomène au premier abord étrange, et, à la réflexion, singulièrement révélateur: une idée peu à peu se fait jour qui, avec saint Bonaventure arrive à son expression achevée: la magnanimité ne se distingue pas de l'humilité, elle n'en est qu'une espèce ou une conséquence" (p. 249).

[29]*Peter Abelard's Ethics. An Edition with Introduction, English Translation and Notes* by D.E. Luscombe (Oxford, 1971).

[30]*Ethics*, p. 14, 14: Ut denique pateat in talibus ipsam quoque voluntatem vel desiderium faciendi quod non licet nequaquam dici peccatum, sed ipsum potius, ut diximus consensum.

[31]*Ethics*, p. 4, 29: Hunc vero consensum proprie peccatum nominamus.

[32]*Ethics*, p. 12, 19: eum ipse (scil. Deus) animum potius quam actionem in remuneratione penset, nec quicquam ad meritum actio addat.

[33]*Ethics*, p. 22, 32: Nichil ergo ad augmentum peccati pertinet qualiscumque operum executio, et nichil animam nisi quod ipsius est coinquinat, hoc est consensus quem solummodo peccatum esse diximus, non voluntatem eum precedentem vel actionem operis subsequentem.

formance of external acts depends upon many factors which are independent of our will; but the internal decision fully depends upon each individual, even when various kinds of pressure act upon him. Abelard adopts the same view with respect to emotions. Whatever desires may occur in an individual, they cannot be termed moral faults. The desire to have sexual intercourse with a woman outside marriage is not in itself a moral fault, but rather consent to this desire.[34] Apparently he regards these emotional tendencies as irrational, as they had been viewed by the Stoics. Such tendencies can never of themselves constitute moral fault. Moral behavior is entirely reduced to the internal attitude of an individual agent. No moral relevance whatsoever is assigned either to emotional tendencies or to the external performance of an act.[35]

Abelard's doctrine is clearly related to Stoic ethics, although the context within which this teaching appears is very different in the two cases. For the Stoics the internal character of moral behavior is connected with their teaching on fate. They maintain, in contrast with the traditional view, that fate is in no way blind or irrational. It coincides with divine Reason which governs the entire development of the world and its history. As a consequence, man is unable to change in any way the course of events. Whatever he does, history pursues its course; for it is constantly determined by immanent divine Reason. Abelard does not accept this kind of external determinism. Therefore, his emphasis on consent as the only relevant factor in moral behavior has a different meaning. He does not claim that man is unable to interfere with the course of events, but rather that insofar as any such intervention is external, it has no moral relevance. Even without any such intervention, the inner act retains its moral quality. On this point there was some disagreement between Abelard and Peter Lombard. The Lombard maintained that certain acts are intrinsically wrong. The subject's intention can never make them morally right.[36]

In Abelard's *Dialogues* it is noteworthy that the Philosopher in the main develops Stoic views in his discussion with his Christian and Jewish interlocutors. He repeatedly mentions natural law as a

---

[34] *Ethics*, p. 12, 44.
[35] *Ethics*, p. 12, 34.
[36] *Ethics*, Introduction, p. xxxvi.

Ethical Perspectives

guide for moral behavior, and stresses that already by observing natural law men may be saved.[37] This remains so even after the promulgation of the Jewish and Christian Laws. At least for some, observance of natural law is enough, without their following other external legal rules.[38] The Philosopher also emphasizes the point that virtue alone can make man happy and that it is sufficient by itself to secure this happiness.[39] As regards the unity of moral life, he insists that it is impossible for one to be moral if one lacks even a single virtue.[40] Like so many other positions which he develops, these views show that the Philosopher's main inspiration is Stoic.

Among twelfth-century authors, mention must also be made of Peter Lombard. His Book of *Sentences* would become the basic text for theology faculties during the Scholastic period. In one of his discussions he refers to a passage where St. Jerome speaks of συντήρησις, a term used by the Greeks. Jerome expresses this in Latin as *scintilla conscientiae*.[41] Instead of literally reproducing the same expression, Peter Lombard speaks rather of *scintilla rationis*.[42] The interest manifested by medieval authors in synderesis springs largely

---

[37] *Dialogus inter Philosophum, Judaeum et Christianum*, ed. R. Thomas (Stuttgart–Bad Cannstatt, 1970), p. 62, 569: Etsi concederemus nunc quoque more priorum sanctorum homines salvari posse sola naturali lege; cf. p. 53, 332.

[38] *Dialogus*, p. 58, 473: Quaero etiam, si nunc quoque post legem vobis datam, sicut et antea, lex naturalis aliquibus sufficere possit absque videlicet exterioribus illis et propriis legis operibus. Quod quidem nulla ratione denegare potestis . . .

[39] *Dialogus*, p. 115, 1969: Nulla quippe his, qui naturalem amplectuntur legem, sententia firmior habetur, quam ut virtus ad beatitudinem sufficiat et quod sole faciunt virtutes beatum, nulla alia quisquam via hoc nomen adipiscitur; p. 100, 1571.

[40] *Dialogus*, p. 108, 1767: Multis namque philosophorum visum est omnibus bonis hominibus omnes simul inesse virtutes nec eum ullatenus bonum censeri, cui virtus aliqua desit, ac per hoc omnium bonorum hominum nec in meritis vite nec in beatitudinis remuneratione ullam esse distantiam. Abelard refers to Cicero, *De officiis*, II, 9–10.

[41] Hieronymus, *In librum Ezechielis*, I, c. 1 (*PL* 25, 22). He is dealing with the fourth part of the soul: Quartamque possunt quae super haec et extra haec tria sunt, quam Graeci vocant synteresin, quae scintilla conscientiae in Cain quoque pectore, postquam eiectus est de paradiso, non extinguitur.

[42] Petrus Lombardus, *Liber Sententiarum*, II, dist. 39: Superior enim scintilla rationis, quae etiam, ut ait Hieronymus, *Super Ezechielem*, c. 1, in Cain non potuit extingui, bonum semper vult, et malum semper odit.

from Peter Lombard's work, which was constantly read and commented upon. Philip the Chancellor was the first medieval writer to devote a special treatise to this topic, in which he used the formula *potentia habitualis*.[43] Beginning with Alexander of Hales, two different interpretations of synderesis were gradually developed, one by the Franciscans, and another by the Dominicans. According to Bonaventure, synderesis is a natural impulse (*pondus naturale*) which inclines the will to what is right.[44] Albert the Great, under the influence of Philip the Chancellor, speaks of a faculty that provides us with habitual knowledge of the principles of natural law.[45] Thomas Aquinas also understands synderesis as a *habitus* of the first principles of practical reason.[46]

Hence the question may be raised concerning the origins of this central notion. Many studies have already been devoted to this. Without entering into details, I would say that present research shows that the term synderesis, or at least the doctrine connected with it, springs from Stoicism. In fact this, together with natural law and conscience, is one of the three most important Stoic notions introduced into the moral teaching of the Middle Ages. One may point to the analogy between the Ciceronian pair *conscientia-conservatio* and the Thomistic pair *conscientia-synderesis*. The term *conservatio* could be the Latin translation of συντήρησις. In Cicero the term *conservatio* signifies certain fundamental demands of nature in general and of human nature in particular. The Greek term was probably used by certain authors close to Panaetius.[47]

It might be more important, however, to show that the doctrine

---

[43]O. Lottin, *Psychologie et morale aux XIIe et XIIIe siècles*, T. II: *Problèmes de morale*, première partie (Louvain-Gembloux, 1948), pp. 138–57.

[44]Bonaventura, *Sent.* II, dist. 39, a. 1, q. 1 (ed. Quaracchi, t. 2, p. 916).

[45]Albertus, *Summa de homine*, q. 71, a. 1 ad 3 (*Opera omnia*, ed. Borgnet, t. 35, p. 593).

[46]Thomas, *De Ver.*, q. 16, a. 1 in c.: habitus naturalis primorum principiorum operabilium, quae sunt universalia principia iuris naturalis. Regarding the use of the term synderesis, M.B. Crowe writes: "It is clear then, that, by the time he came to write his *Summa Theologiae*, St. Thomas no longer regarded *synderesis* as a term of importance" (*The Changing Profile of the Natural Law* [The Hague, 1977], p. 140).

[47]J. Hebing, "Ueber *conscientia* und *conservatio* im philosophischen Sinne bei den Römern von Cicero bis Hieronymus," *Philosophisches Jahrbuch* 35 (1922), pp. 136–52, 215–31, 301–26. I want to refer particularly to p. 326.

connected with synderesis should be seen in relation to the teaching on *oikeiosis*. This term refers to the basic impulse of a being, especially of man, toward himself, toward his own nature and condition, toward what is suitable and connatural for him, in a word, toward whatever is appropriate for him.[48] According to the Stoics *oikeiosis* is the starting point for moral life. Corresponding to *oikeiosis*, the medieval *synderesis* expresses the precise content, the meaning and orientation, of this basic impulse.[49] The two Greek terms (*oikeiosis* and *synderesis*) and the two Latin terms (*conciliatio* and *conservatio*) seem to have influenced one another linguistically so as finally to become synonyms.[50]

With this in mind, one can easily understand how two different interpretations of synderesis (the voluntarist and the intellectualist) developed in the thirteenth century. The Stoic *oikeiosis* is so fundamental that it lies beyond the distinction between mind and will. Even Aquinas, though he presents an intellectualist interpretation of this term, recognizes and repeatedly states that the human will is naturally orientated toward the good and always strives toward whatever it seeks under the aspect of the good. Not only does Stoic teaching about *oikeiosis* correspond to medieval discussions of synderesis, but so, too, does Stoic thinking about natural anticipations (προλήψεις) and common notions (κοιναὶ ἔννοιαι).[51]

If our analysis is correct, then one must admit that Stoicism's influence on medieval ethics was very profound indeed. The doctrine of synderesis is not marginal, but at the very center of moral philosophy and moral theology. What does it mean exactly? First of all, it means that moral life is not an alienation, not imposed on man

---

[48]Diog. Laërtios, VII, 85 (*SVF* III, 178).
[49]Cicero, *De finibus*, III, 5, 16: Placet his, quorum ratio mihi probatur, simul atque natum sit animal ipsum sibi conciliari et commendari ad se conservandum et ad suum statum eaque quae conservantia sunt eius status diligenda. S.G. Pembroke ("*Oikeiosis*," in *Problems in Stoicism*, ed. A.A. Long [London, 1971], pp. 114–49) writes in his study on *oikeiosis*: "If there had been no *oikeiosis*, there would have been no Stoa" (pp. 114–15).
[50]J.R. Moncho Pascual, "La doctrina de la razon practica segun Santo Tomas," doctoral dissertation (Valencia, 1975), p. 50.
[51]J.R. Moncho Pascual, *op. cit.*, p. 50: "Y asi en conclusion, el termino escolastico de 'synderesis', o en todo caso, la doctrina subyacente, nos parece ser una pervivencia o revivencia de la 'oikeiosis', doctrina basica de la ética estoica."

from without, not a constraint that is contrary to man's nature. Moral behavior rather corresponds to the basic orientation of the individual human being, and conforms to what is truly of value for him. In some circumstances ethical behavior may be difficult. But within the framework of this teaching it remains true that only a moral life constitutes man's true perfection. Moreover, the teaching on synderesis implies that everyone grasps by intuition the basic rules and principles of morality, even without any special training. Moral life is the same everywhere and for everyone. Of course, its basic principles must be specified further, and in this respect many different kinds of rules may be introduced. But according to this view, at least the basic moral intuitions are the same in all men and at all times. Finally, the notion of synderesis takes on special importance in a Christian context. According to Christian belief original sin is present in every human being. All humans bear in their nature the consequences of sinfulness going back to the beginnings of mankind. This teaching was accepted and developed by Christians. In spite of the fall, however, the doctrine of synderesis means that man continues to be inclined in a fundamental way to moral perfection.

Closely connected with synderesis is the topic of natural law. Here again the influence of Stoicism is readily discerned. The distinction between civil law and natural law was clearly drawn by Isidore of Seville. While civil law differs from one country to another, natural law is the same for all peoples.[52] This universal character is an important feature of natural law. It will constantly be emphasized by later medieval authors, and corresponds to authentic Stoic teaching on the same matter. Since there is one divine Reason which permeates the entire universe, there is only one fundamental moral rule for all human beings, wherever they may live. Without necessarily being at variance with this fundamental law, positive legislation may differ in various countries. Nonetheless, civil law always has its roots in the fundamental principles of natural law.

The Roman jurist Gaius (second century) holds the same position, but uses different terminology. Instead of speaking of natural

---

[52]*Isidori Hispalensis Episcopi Etymologiorum sive originum libri XX*, ed. Lindsay (Oxford, 1911), V, 4: Jus naturale est commune omnium nationum, et quod ubique instinctu naturae, non constitutione aliqua habeatur ut viri et feminae conjunctio, librorum susceptio et educatio, communis omnium possessio et omnium una libertas, acquisitio eorum quae caelo, terra marique capiuntur. Item depositae rei vel commodatae restitutio.

law, he uses the expression *ius gentium*, or the law of nations. In his view, this law is based on natural reason. It is accepted and practiced by all nations. It is clear that for Gaius the law of nations is not to be understood as positive law.[53] In this respect there is a difference between Gaius and Isidore. The latter speaks of the law of nations rather in the sense of positive legislation.[54] Ulpian introduces a new distinction between natural law and the law of nations. The first is common both to man and animals. The second applies to man alone, though it is the same in all countries and for all peoples.[55] Ulpian's definition of natural law must be understood against the background of a question frequently raised in antiquity: do animals also have certain rights? In other words, is there a juridical order that includes not only humans but animals? Ulpian's definition implies that rights extend both to humans and to animals.[56] Justinian, on the other hand, reproduces Ulpian's view of natural law, but at the same time proposes a definition of the law of nations which corresponds to that of Gaius.[57] Given all of this, we may conclude that the law of nations is used somewhat ambiguously. While Gaius and Justinian view it as a kind of natural law, Ulpian and Saint Isidore rather define it as positive. This ambiguity is felt

---

[53]Gaius, *Digesta*, 41, 1, 1: Quarumdam rerum dominium nanciscimur iure gentium, quod ratione naturali inter omnes homines peraeque servatur; quarumdam iure civili, i.e. iure proprio civitatis nostrae. . . . Et quia antiquius ius gentium cum ipso genere humano proditum est . . .
[54]*Etymologiorum libri*, V, 6: Ius gentium est sedum occupatio, munitio, bella, captivitates, postliminia, foedera pacis, induciae, legatorum non violandorum religio, connubia inter alienegenas prohibita; et inde ius gentium, quo eo iure fere omnes gentes utuntur.
[55]*Dig.*, I, 1, 1, 3: Jus naturale est quod natura omnia animalia docuit. Nam istud jus non humani generis proprium, sed omnium animalium quae in terra, quae in mari nascuntur, avium quoque commune est. Hinc descendit maris atque feminae conjunctio, quam nos matrimonium appellamus; hinc liberorum procreatio, hinc educatio; videmus enim coetera quoque animalia, feras etiam, istius juris peritia censeri. Jus gentium est quo gentes humanae utuntur; quod a naturali recedere facile intelligere licet, quia illud omnibus animalibus, hoc solis hominibus inter se commune sit.
[56]According to the Stoics there is no moral or juridical relation between men and animals since the latter are not endowed with reason. Cf. M. Pohlenz, *Die Stoa, Geschichte einer geistigen Bewegung*, 2 vols. (Göttingen, 1948), I, p. 137.
[57]Cf. O. Lottin, *Le droit naturel chez saint Thomas d'Aquin et ses prédécesseurs*, 2nd ed. (Bruges, 1931), p. 8.

even in the writings of Aquinas, who was forced to devote two different articles to the law of nations—two articles which, at least at first sight, appear to stand in contradiction with one another.[58]

From the twelfth century onward the doctrine of natural law was developed further. As might be expected, some features of the original Stoic teaching on natural law were completely transformed. Within the Stoic framework there is a close connection between pantheism and natural law. *Physis* coincides with the immanent Divine Reason. This perspective was abandoned by Christian theology, for which God's transcendence is an important issue. Moreover, the content of natural law received a new inspiration from Christian belief. According to Hugh of St. Victor, natural law contains two fundamental rules for conduct: Behave towards others as you would have them behave toward yourself. Do not do to others that which you would not have them do to you. This maxim does not come from Stoic sources, even though the Stoics professed universal concern for fellow man. It clearly comes instead from Christianity. Both of these rules were introduced into the *Decretum Gratiani*, where they are viewed as belonging to nature.[59]

Abelard is also familiar with the doctrine of natural law. Since natural law is based on human reason and since this is common to all men, so too is natural law itself universal. According to this position, certain basic moral intuitions are the same everywhere and in all periods of history.[60] The commentators on the *Decretum Gratiani* generally regard natural law as a kind of fundamental inclination in man to do what is right and to avoid what is wrong.[61]

---

[58]Aquinas follows Isidore in the *Summa Theologiae*, I–II, q. 95, a. 4 in c.: Dividitur ius positivum in ius gentium et ius civile. But in the *Summa Theologiae*, II–II, q. 57, a. 3 in c., he adopts the position of Gaius to whom he explicitly refers: Quod . . . naturalis ratio inter omnes homines constituit, id apud omnes peraeque custoditur, vocaturque ius gentium . . . (*Dig.*, I, 1, 9).

[59]Cf. O. Lottin, *Psychologie et morale aux XIIe et XIIIe siècles*, II, 1, pp. 72–73.

[60]*Dialogus*, ed. Thomas, p. 124, 2220: Ius quippe aliud naturale, aliud positivum dicitur. Naturale quidem ius est quod opere complendum esse ipsa, que omnibus naturaliter inest, ratio persuadet, et idcirco apud omnes permanet, ut Deum colere. . . . Positivae autem iustitie illud est, quod ab hominibus constitutum.

[61]Cf. *Die Summa decretorum des Magister Rufinus*, ed. Singer (Pader-

Ethical Perspectives

This viewpoint corresponds to the Stoics' teaching about *oikeiosis*. According to them, man is by nature inclined to do what is appropriate for him. One of the Decretists, Simon of Bosiniano, identified natural law with synderesis. By this he means to say that it is an inborn intuition of the first principles for moral behavior. Because this insight is part of man's natural equipment, it can never be extinguished—not even in Cain.[62] In this usage the term "natural" in the expression "natural law" refers to the way in which man grasps the basic principles of moral conduct. He does not have to learn them. He knows them without special training. Joannes Teutonicus maintains a similar position. Along with other possible meanings, natural law may be taken as referring to the commandments of the Decalogue, which are immediately connected with human reason.[63]

In summarizing twelfth-century teaching on natural law, one may say that it is thought to be a universal rule, one and the same for all peoples and at all times. Whatever differences may exist in the area of positive legislation, all are related to some fundamental principles which are the same everywhere. Moreover, natural law refers either to a natural inclination to moral behavior, or to an inborn knowledge of basic moral principles. In any event, "natural" in the expression "natural law" does not mean physical. It has nothing to do with physics, and above all, not in the modern sense of this term. Most medieval writers do not regard man as a merely physical being. He is both physical and meta-physical.

In the thirteenth century new questions were raised concerning natural law, especially the issue of its immutability. Is natural law an unchangeable norm for moral life, or does it change in the course of history? This question did not arise within a Stoic context, nor was it directly connected with Stoic sources. It has to do with the reflec-

---

born, 1902), 6: est naturale ius vis quedam humane creature a natura insita ad faciendum bonum cavendumque contrarium (cf. O. Lottin, *Psychologie et morale*, II, 1, p. 74).

[62]Cf. O. Lottin, *Psychologie et morale*, II, 1, p. 74: The following passage is quoted from a Bamberg manuscript: Nobis itaque videtur quod ius naturale est superior pars anime, ipsa videlicet ratio que sinderesis appellatur, que nec in Chain potuit, scriptura teste, extingui. Cum autem sit natura, id est naturale bonum, delictorum meritis offuscari potuit, nunquam extingui (*Bamberg Staatsbibl. Can.* 38, f. 2ra).

[63]Cf. O. Lottin, *Psychologie et morale*, II, 1, pp. 74–75.

tions of Christian theologians on natural law. In studying the history of the Chosen People, these writers had to face the problem whether the behavior of the most eminent Old Testament figures was in conformity with natural law. This gave rise to the question concerning the changeable or unchangeable character of natural law. Is it possible that certain kinds of behavior which were permitted in the past are no longer legitimate? The Stoics constantly emphasize the general and universal character of natural law. It is the same everywhere and for all human beings. Does it remain the same throughout the course of history? This question does not really matter for the Stoics. The entire development of history is the work of the immanent Divine Law, and man has to live in conformity with it.

As regards thirteenth-century Christian writers, many of their texts concerning natural law have been gathered together by O. Lottin. For instance, at the beginning of that century William of Auxerre incorporated the doctrine of natural law into theology since, for him, this law is the origin and principle of all moral virtues.[64] It refers to those rules of moral conduct which natural reason lays down and, as a consequence, applies only to beings endowed with reason.[65] According to William, there is a parallel between speculative knowledge and practical knowledge. Just as the first principles of speculative thought are immediately evident, so too are the first principles of practical reason. In both areas there must be some primary knowledge that is immediately evident. In other words, not every statement can be proved from higher principles.[66] With respect to the content of natural law, William distinguishes between rules of first necessity and others which are of second necessity. Only the first type are in all circumstances required for man to attain his final end. For William this group includes monogamy, an issue that became rather controversial.[67]

---

[64]Cf. O. Lottin, *Psychologie et morale*, II, 1, p. 75.
[65]Guilelmus of Auxerre, *Summa aurea in quattuor libros sententiarum* (Paris, 1500), f. 287 ra: Ius naturale speciale est quod dictat naturalis ratio, et tale ius est in utentibus ratione.
[66]Cf. O. Lottin, *Psychologie et morale*, II, 1, p. 76: Sicut in speculativis sunt quedam que per se sunt nota, que sunt pura natura speculationis, ita in agendis sunt quedam principia agendi per se nota in quibus ius nature consistit (Guilelmus of Auxerre, *Summa aurea*, f. 66 ra).
[67]Cf. O. Lottin, *Psychologie et morale*, II, 1, p. 76.

Ethical Perspectives 61

Philip the Chancellor uses a different vocabulary and distinguishes between *ius naturae ut natura* and *ius naturae ut ratio*. The first is more restricted than the second. As regards marriage, the first part of natural law merely prescribes that the human species be propagated; but the second part includes monogamy. It is in this way that Philip accounts for the behavior of the Old Testament Patriarchs.[68]

In an anonymous work, *De lege naturali*, the question is raised whether natural law is to be viewed as an act or as a habit (*habitus*). The anonymous writer replies that it is both. It is an act of reason because reason, owing to a natural intuition, dictates how man is to behave. It is also a disposition of the will because the will has a natural inclination to do what reason ordains. In this way this writer presents an interpretation of natural law which is both intellectualistic and voluntaristic.[69]

Guerric of St. Quentin, a Dominican Master, adopts the same position. At the same time, however, he denies that natural law includes all the commandments of the Decalogue. It is confined to reason's most fundamental moral intuitions.[70]

Roland of Cremona also distinguishes between primary and immutable precepts, and others which are secondary and changeable. Like Philip the Chancellor, he appeals to this distinction in order to account for certain practices recorded in the Bible.[71] He identifies natural law with the natural inclination of all beings to the good. In man this inclination coincides with synderesis. Thus Philip

---

[68] Cf. O. Lottin, *Psychologie et morale*, II, 1, p. 77.

[69] Cf. O. Lottin, *Psychologie et morale*, II, 1, p. 78. According to the author a law always implies an act of judging and commanding. If there is no formal judgment imposing a particular way of conduct, there is no law. Consequently natural law must also include this factor and be an act of reason.

[70] O. Lottin (*Psychologie et morale*, II, 1, pp. 84–85) quotes a passage from a Vatican manuscript (*Vat. lat.* 4245 f. 63 vb): Non est autem lex naturalis potentia, sed actus rationis. Sed magis videtur quod habitus informativus, cum dictum sit paulo ante quod est sententia rationis non actualis sed est naturalis et est nichilominus habitus voluntatis; est enim lex ista rationis sicut imperatoris vel imponentis, voluntatis autem sicut populi et cui imponitur.

[71] A.H. Chroust, "The Philosophy of Law from St. Augustine to St. Thomas Aquinas," *The New Scholasticism* 20 (1946), pp. 26–71; on p. 43 the author refers to a Paris manuscript, *Bibl. Mazarine*, Cod. 795.

can state that synderesis itself is natural law (*ipsa sinderesis est ius naturale*).[72] So understood, synderesis comes close to the Stoic notion of *oikeiosis*.

Albert the Great does not agree with Ulpian's definition of natural law. According to Albert this law holds only for humans, not for animals.[73] His teaching on natural law is in agreement with that of William of Auxerre. Natural law includes the first principles of practical reason and their immediate consequences; but all kinds of positive laws are specified and elaborated by man. These are not universally valid; they are not the same in every country; and they are not independent from the more fundamental principles of moral conduct, even though they do not immediately follow from them.[74] Here mention must also be made of Albert's teaching about the practical syllogism. As will be developed below, Albert tries to draw a clear distinction between synderesis and conscience in light of the practical syllogism.[75]

According to John of La Rochelle, there is a natural law. Man does not have to acquire knowledge of this since it is inborn. The content of natural law corresponds to that of the Decalogue. This is not to imply, however, that natural law and the Ten Commandments simply coincide. The Decalogue implies a supernatural motive—charity—and is directed toward a supernatural ultimate end.[76] John obviously wants to show that there is no opposition between the fundamental moral precepts as they are grasped naturally and the Ten Commandments; but he also wishes to safeguard the supernatural character of Revelation.

Alexander of Hales distinguishes three kinds of natural law. First there is what he names *ius nativum*. This applies to acts which are common to men and animals. Secondly, *ius humanum* is concerned

---

[72] O. Lottin, *Psychologie et morale*, II, 1, p. 83; *Le droit naturel*, pp. 40ff.; note 125.

[73] M.B. Crowe, *The Changing Profile of the Natural Law* (The Hague, 1977), pp. 120–22; Albertus, *Summa de bono*, Tract. V, "De iustitia," q. 1, a. 1 (*Opera omnia*, XXVIII [Münster, 1951], pp. 265–66): Non enim consentimus in distinctionem quam quidam posuerunt, scil. quod ius naturale multis modis dicatur, et uno modo sit commune nobis cum brutis.

[74] O. Lottin, *Psychologie et morale*, II, 1, p. 85; *Le droit naturel*, pp. 116–19.

[75] *Summa de creaturis*, II, q. 72, a. 1 (*Opera omnia*, ed. Borgnet, t. 35, p. 599).

[76] O. Lottin, *Psychologie et morale*, II, 1, pp. 86–87.

Ethical Perspectives

with distinctively human behavior. Finally, *ius divinum* applies to these same actions (those that are distinctively human), but as related to grace. According to Alexander, the specifically human law is a natural dictate of reason (*naturale dictamen rationis*). This means that man can know these fundamental moral principles without the help of Revelation.[77]

Bonaventure formulates three definitions of natural law: first, that which is found in the Old Testament and the Gospels; secondly, that which is common to all nations; and thirdly, that which belongs to the nature of all living beings. Bonaventure regards this third definition as the most appropriate.[78] Since he holds that synderesis is the faculty of reason endowed with habitual knowledge of the first principles of moral life, Bonaventure's interpretation is not purely voluntaristic.[79]

In his Commentary on the *Sentences*, Thomas Aquinas states that the first principles of practical reason constitute natural law. Since man is equipped with reason, he is not guided by natural impulse in his behavior but by a rational intuition of natural law, that is, by *ratio naturalis*.[80] Like William of Auxerre, Aquinas emphasizes the parallel between speculative and practical reason. There are certain basic principles in speculative science which are not acquired in the strict sense but which are to some extent innate (they belong to the original structure of the human mind, even though they could not be known without the aid of experience). So too, there must be some fundamental principles in the field of practical reason.[81] The argumentation developed for this by Aquinas is similar to that which he offers in order to prove the existence of an Unmoved Mover. If all knowledge presupposes and rests on prior knowledge, it will be impossible for us to know anything with certainty. At least some fundamental principles must be self-evident. These serve as the foundation on which all other knowledge is based. These fundamen-

---

[77]O. Lottin, *Psychologie et morale*, II, 1, pp. 88–89.

[78]Bonaventura, *In IV Sent.*, d. 33, a. 1, q. 1 (*Opera omnia*, ed. Quaracchi, t. 4, 1889, p. 748).

[79]Bonaventura, *In II Sent.*, d. 39, a. 2, q. 1 (*Opera omnia*, t. 2, p. 910).

[80]*In IV Sent.*, d. 33, q. 1, a. 1.

[81]*Summa Theologiae*, I–II, q. 94, a. 2: Sicut autem ens est primum quod cadit in apprehensione simpliciter, ita bonum est primum quod cadit in apprehensione practicae rationis, quae ordinatur ad opus: omne enim agens agit propter finem, qui habet rationem boni.

tal principles are the very content of natural law, and are known by synderesis.

In his *Summa Theologiae* Aquinas returns to this issue. Natural law, like all law, must be viewed as an *ordinatio rationis* (ordinance of reason).[82] Consequently, natural law is not a *habitus* properly speaking and cannot, without qualification, be identified with synderesis. Natural law is the object of synderesis in this sense that principles of moral life are present in man in habitual fashion.[83] Moreover, natural law must be understood as a participation in eternal law, which is present in all beings gifted with reason. In accord with the Stoic notion of *oikeiosis* Aquinas also speaks of certain natural inclinations which are present in each individual and correspond to the various levels of his essential makeup. These include an individual's inclination to preserve his own being, another inclination which corresponds to his nature as an animal, and finally, one which follows from his rational nature.[84] In this sense moral life entirely corresponds to the fundamental tendencies of a human being. According to Aquinas, natural law not only includes the very first principles of moral behavior, but also the consequences which immediately flow from them. Thus there are positive and negative precepts which are more or less closely related to the first principles. Aquinas distinguishes, for instance, between polyandry and polygamy. Prohibition of the first is much more closely connected with basic moral principles than is prohibition of the second.[85]

According to Peter of Tarentaise, natural law in the strict sense applies only to rational beings such as man. With respect to human behavior, practical reason must be endowed with fundamental moral intuitions. These are precisely what is meant by natural law. Hence, from the first moment of his existence, man bears within himself the seeds of moral life. These will only gradually be developed.[86]

---

[82]*Summa Theologiae*, I-II, q. 90, a. 1.
[83]*Summa Theologiae*, I-II, q. 94, a. 1.
[84]*Summa Theologiae*, I-II, q. 94, a. 2: Tertio modo inest homini inclinatio ad bonum secundum naturam rationis, quae est sibi propria: sicut homo habet naturalem inclinationem ad hoc quod veritatem cognoscat de Deo, et ad hoc quod in societate vivat.
[85]*Summa Theologiae*, I-II, q. 94, a. 2.
[86]O. Lottin, *Psychologie et morale*, II, 1, pp. 93-94.

Ethical Perspectives

In his teaching on natural law Duns Scotus emphasizes divine omnipotence and divine freedom in creating. Natural law is immediately related to the nature of particular beings which in their essential structure have been freely produced by God. Consequently, natural law itself depends upon God's free choice insofar as the kinds of created beings were decided upon by him.[87] According to Scotus, natural law includes both immediately evident practical principles and the consequences that flow from them. Contrary to Aquinas, Scotus acknowledges that God has repeatedly freed certain individuals from particular commandments of the Decalogue. Hence Scotus concludes that these commandments should not be included within the most fundamental principles of natural law.[88] In spite of this difference, both authors agree that God cannot dispense anyone from fulfilling natural law. What matters is to determine which commandments from the Decalogue are necessary for man to attain his final end. According to Scotus the commandments from the Second Tablet are not first principles; nor are they necessarily connected with first principles.[89]

William of Ockham's teaching on natural law reveals the same orientation as that of Duns Scotus. William also stresses divine power and divine freedom in creating. The distinction between what is morally right and morally wrong is determined by the divine will. From the fact that God wills something we may conclude that it is right to act accordingly. Divorce is morally wrong because God has forbidden it. If God had commanded it, it would then be morally right. Thus, if God commanded someone to hate him, this action

---

[87] M.B. Crowe, *The Changing Profile*, pp. 196–98; p. 198: "But if law is a matter of will rather than reason and if will, further, must be radically free, then the problem takes on another aspect. In this case human nature provides a *lex mere indicans*, which falls short of the true concept of law; the scale of good and evil, determined by comparison with human nature must wait upon God's will which, by imposing it, makes it a *lex obstringens.*"

[88] *Ox.*, IV, d. 26, q. un., n. 7: Propriissime de lege naturae est principium practicum per se notum et conclusio demonstrative descendens ex tali principio; secundario autem de lege naturae est verum evidenter consonum talibus principiis et conclusionibus licet non necessario sequens.

[89] According to Scotus the divine will could not be determined by anything outside itself. Cf. M.B. Crowe, *The Changing Profile*, p. 200: "To hold that human nature can determine God's will is, according to Scotus, to fall into the error of the philosophers."

would then be good.⁹⁰ This does not mean, however, that in the present moral order divorce or killing or hatred of God could ever be morally right. Ockham's point is that the moral order in which we live depends upon God's choice. Absolutely speaking, God could have prescribed a different moral order. "Natural law is for him positive law, divine will. . . . Law is will, sheer will without any *fundamentum in re* in the essential nature."⁹¹ Ockham holds that man must live in accord with reason. This means that man should orientate his life in accord with the moral order that has been freely decided upon by God.

By way of résumé, one may summarize the preceding survey by singling out certain characteristic features of medieval teaching on natural law which betray Stoic influence:

1. There is a supreme law that serves as the basic norm for moral conduct.

2. This law coincides with reason. The meaning of "reason" is not, of course, the same in Stoic philosophy and in medieval thought.

3. Natural law is universal. It is the same for all nations, while positive laws differ from country to country.

4. Natural law is immutable, at least in its most fundamental principles. This point was frequently discussed by medieval thinkers because of the behavior of important representatives of the Chosen People as recorded in the Old Testament. Apparently such actions were not condemned by Jahweh, although they could hardly be reconciled with natural law.

5. Natural law is the foundation for every moral or legal prescription, and corresponds to a fundamental inclination in every individual human being.

---

[90]M.B. Crowe, *The Changing Profile*, pp. 201ff. The author notes that several recent studies have mitigated the traditional interpretation of Ockham and have introduced a more balanced view of his doctrine. Ockham uses the term natural law in his political writings, but not in his ethical and theological works. Why not? Referring to an article of K. McDonnell ("Does William of Ockham have a Theory of Natural Law?" *Franciscan Studies* 34 [1974], pp. 383-92) Crowe mentions two reasons: "(1) the idea of 'nature' posed problems for Ockham who found it a limitation upon freedom; and (2) Ockham propounded a personalist ethics in which 'nature' could only figure as an unnecessary link between God and man" (p. 203).

[91]Cf. H. Rommen, *Die ewige Wiederkehr des Naturrechts*, 2nd ed. (Munich, 1927), p. 60.

6. Natural law is known by an inborn intuition that is present in all men without special education or training.

In addition to synderesis and natural law, there is still another notion of Stoic origin that plays an important role in medieval ethics, that is to say, *syneidesis* or conscience. Seneca, who was well known to the Latin West, exercised decisive influence on this matter. According to M. Pohlenz, Seneca was the first philosopher who fully appreciated the meaning of moral conscience.[92] In his dialogue *De ira* he reports that he usually examined himself every evening. He would call himself to the court of his own conscience, and would submit all that he had done during the day to its judgment.[93] In a recent study A. Cancrini, in opposition to C.A. Pierce's interpretation,[94] maintains that the notion of conscience is present in Stoic teaching at the various stages of that school's development, and especially in Panaetius, Posidonius, and the later representatives.[95]

There was probably some connection between the notion of conscience and the doctrine of moral progress. During the early stage of Stoic philosophy, mankind was divided into two groups, a very small group of wise men, and the enormous mass of the unwise. Immoral people can reach wisdom or moral perfection, but this transition is not gradual or step by step but sudden. So long as an individual does not possess all moral virtues, he belongs to the unwise.[96] Chrysippus already presents a more flexible position, owing to the notion of *officium* or duty. Duty holds an intermediary position between perfect moral action and moral fault.[97] An indi-

---

[92]*Die Stoa. Geschichte einer geistigen Bewegung* (Göttingen, 1948), p. 317: "Es ist für uns das erste Mal in der griechisch-römischen Philosophie, dass das Gewissen in dieser Weise als lebendige Macht gewürdigt wird."

[93]*De ira*, III, 36: Utor hac potestate et cotidie apud me causam dico. Cum sublatum e conspectu lumen est et conticuit uxor moris iam mei conscia, totum diem meum scrutor factaque ac dicta mea remetior: nihil mihi ipse abscondo, nihil transeo. Talking about his habit of examining his conscience every day before going to sleep, Seneca refers to the example of A. Sextius, whose teaching was a synthesis of Stoic and Pythagorean elements. The practice of a daily examination of conscience further dates back to the School of Pythagoras.

[94]*Conscience in the New Testament*, 2nd ed. (London, 1958).

[95]A. Cancrini, *Syneidesis. Il tema semantico della "con-scientia" nella Grecia antica* (Rome, 1970), p. 150.

[96]Plutarchus, *Quomodo quis suos in virtute sentiat profectus*, 75 c.

[97]Stobaeus, *Ecl.*, II, 85, 13 (*SVF* III, 494); Cicero, *De finibus*, III, 17, 58 (*SVF* III, 498).

vidual who faithfully fulfills his daily duties is at the threshold of wisdom. Being aware of his faults in words and actions, he constantly makes progress towards moral perfection.[98] This doctrine of moral progress was developed further by Panaetius and Posidonius. According to the latter, not two but three different groups of people are to be distinguished. In addition to the wise and the unwise, many are neither completely wise nor really immoral. They belong to an intermediate group, and are progressing towards virtue.[99] Within this context of moral progress, conscience plays a decisive role. Because of his conscience, each individual is constantly aware of the point he has already reached, and of what is still lacking to him. Without the permanent control of conscience, moral progress would not be possible.

In medieval thought the notion of conscience was not always clearly defined. It was sometimes identified with natural law, or with synderesis, or even with free choice.[100] Philip the Chancellor attempts to distinguish between conscience and synderesis. While conscience deals with concrete particular situations, synderesis is concerned with universal moral principles. Moreover, while knowledge of universal moral principles is not fallible, conscience may be mistaken—the application of a general principle to a particular case may be wrong in one way or another. And finally, conscience, being a kind of deliberation, always involves some free choice in its exercise.[101]

Bonaventure also tries to distinguish between conscience and synderesis, but his position clearly differs from that of his predecessor. According to Bonaventure, conscience is a disposition of practical reason. It belongs to the area of moral intuition. Synderesis is rather a desiring power, which strives towards what is good.[102] In considering the precise nature of this moral intuition, Bonaventure states that it is partly innate and partly acquired. Even our knowledge of basic principles could never be totally independent from perception and experience.[103]

---

[98]Proclus, *In Plat. Alcib. pr.*, vol. III, p. 158 ed. Cousin (*SVF* III, 543).

[99]Diog. Laërt., VII, 91. Cf. G. Verbeke, "Les Stoïciens et le progrès de l'histoire," *Revue philos. de Louvain* 62 (1964), pp. 34–35.

[100]M.B. Crowe, *The Changing Profile*, p. 133.

[101]T.C. Potts, *Conscience in Medieval Philosophy* (Cambridge, 1980), pp. 12–20.

[102]T.C. Potts, *Conscience in Medieval Philosophy*, pp. 32–33.

[103]T.C. Potts, *Conscience in Medieval Philosophy*, p. 35: "Arguing

Ethical Perspectives

Faced with this rather fluctuating understanding of conscience, Albert the Great introduced a decisive clarification and a synthesis. He combined the Stoic teaching on synderesis, conscience, and natural law with the Aristotelian doctrine of the practical syllogism as found in the *Nichomachean Ethics*.[104] The major premise of this syllogism is provided by synderesis. It springs from the habitual knowledge of natural law which is present in every individual. In Albert's view, natural law includes the first principles of practical reason and their immediate consequences. This knowledge does not result from learning and education. It is part of the original makeup of an individual human being. The minor premise is the work of reason. A particular case with which a person is confronted is considered in light of a general rule. The conclusion is drawn by conscience, which itself is an act of reason applying a general moral intuition to a particular situation.[105] In this combination, a clear distinction is drawn between synderesis, conscience, and natural law. These three concepts are fundamentally Stoic, but Albert's teaching on the practical syllogism is Aristotelian.

A similar teaching concerning conscience is developed by Thomas Aquinas, who devotes an entire *quaestio* of his *De veritate* to this issue. According to Thomas, conscience is neither a disposition (*habitus*) nor a faculty. It rather designates the actual application of first practical principles to a particular act.[106] Thus conscience is

---

against Philip, he [i.e. Bonaventure] quotes Aristotle to the effect that even our knowledge of basic premises (whether of theoretical or practical reasoning) is acquired from memory, perception and experience."

[104]*Eth. Nic.*, VII, 3, 1146b8ff. The whole chapter deals with the relationship between knowledge and temperance, which is a crucial topic with respect to the moral intellectualism of Socrates. The question asked is whether it is possible that man's behavior does not correspond to his moral knowledge. So Aristotle's inquiry is not concerned with the ἀκόλαστος who acts consciously and deliberately, but with the ἀκράτης, whose judgment remains sound and yet whose behavior is not in conformity with it.

[105]*Summa de creaturis*, II, q. 72, a. 1 (*Opera omnia*, ed. Borgnet, t. 35, p. 599): Dicimus quod conscientia conclusio est rationis practicae ex duobus praemissis, quorum major synderesis et minor rationis. . . . Major autem istius syllogismi est synderesis, cujus est inclinare in bonum per universales rationes boni. Minor vero est rationis cujus est conferre particulare ad universale. Conclusio autem est conscientiae. According to M.B. Crowe the same view is found in the questions *De sinderesi* and *De conscientia*, and also in the *Summa Theologiae* (*The Changing Profile*, p. 134).

[106]*De Veritate*, q. 17, a. 1 in c.: Unde conscientia non potest nominare

regarded as an act of moral insight wherein a particular action, either future or past, is judged in light of basic ethical principles.[107] One of Thomas's main concerns is to determine whether conscience may be mistaken. The starting point of a practical syllogism is some kind of universal knowledge provided by synderesis. This knowledge can never be erroneous. But, according to Aquinas, application of this general insight to a particular case requires an intermediate step, the intervention of either superior or inferior reason. In this step error is possible.[108] Furthermore, the application itself may be done in the wrong way.[109] There are cases, however, where the connection between premises and conclusion is so clear and immediate that any danger of error is eliminated.[110] Thomas, therefore, has also clearly distinguished between synderesis, natural law, and conscience.

In attempting to summarize the preceding survey, I would say that *three* fundamental Stoic notions have deeply influenced medieval moral philosophy and theology. These notions are synderesis, conscience, and natural law. After a period of some hesitation and uncertainty, these notions were combined with Aristotle's teaching about practical reason. This combination resulted in the theory of the practical syllogism as it was developed by Albert the Great and by Thomas Aquinas. In light of the preceding analysis I might also note that natural law as it stems from the Stoics and was developed by medieval thinkers is rather different from what some contemporary moralists understand it to be. As it was worked out in the thirteenth century it became a coherent part of moral doctrine—the result of some fifteen centuries of ethical reflection.

---

aliquem habitum specialem, vel aliquam potentiam, sed nominat ipsum actum, qui est applicatio cuiuscumque habitus vel cuiuscumque notitiae ad aliquem actum particularem.

[107]*De Veritate*, q. 17, a. 1 in c.: Aquinas speaks of a double way (duplex est via): Una secundum quod per habitum scientiae dirigimur in aliquid faciendum vel non faciendum. Alio modo secundum quod actus postquam factus est, examinatur ad habitum scientiae, an sit rectus vel non rectus.

[108]*De Veritate*, q. 17, a. 2 in c.: sed in iudicio rationis superioris contingit esse peccatum. . . . Et similiter contingere potest error in conscientia ex errore existente in inferiore parte rationis.

[109]*De Veritate*, q. 17, a. 2 in c.

[110]*De Veritate*, q. 17, a. 2 in c.: Secundum tamen quod in quibusdam conscientia nunquam errare potest: quando scilicet actus ille particularis ad quem conscientia applicatur, habet de se in synderesi universale iudicium.

CHAPTER IV

FATALISM AND FREEDOM

Belief in the domination of fate dates back to ancient times. The notion of destiny frequently appears in Greek literature and is expressed by various terms. The most tragic symbol of the inexorable power of fate is Prometheus. As he is depicted by Aeschylus, Prometheus—the great benefactor of mankind—is the victim of an unrelenting necessity, to which even the power of divine beings is subordinated. Even Zeus is unable to escape from destiny, for he is less powerful than the Parcae or the Erinyes. Taken in its most radical sense, this belief inevitably leads to the view that human existence is entirely dominated by some higher power to which even the gods are subject.

As they usually do when dealing with common opinions, the Stoics do not simply reject this popular belief. They rather incorporate it into their philosophical system and invest it with a new meaning. Fatalism even becomes one of the central ideas in their interpretation of the cosmos. In his Περὶ φύσεως Zeno, the founder of the Stoic School, writes that fate is a power which moves matter in an immutable way, and that it may be called nature or providence.[1] Fate is identified with the creative fire which animates matter and which determines from within the entire evolution of the world. Consequently, destiny coincides with God, who governs the world as an immanent spirit. Instead of excluding providence, fate itself becomes divine providence.

This doctrine is of course far removed from the original mythological view. Granting that fate coincides with immanent divine Reason, Zeno actually follows a path that had already been prepared by Heraclitus. This transposition of popular belief is both bold and radical. In the final analysis it maintains that the world is a perfect work of divine Reason. What people regard as evil is not really such. The only real evil is to abandon the divine law and to act

---

[1]Aëtius, I, 27, 5 (D D G, p. 322b9); Theodoretus, *Graec. aff. cur.*, VI, 14, p. 153 Ra. (*SVF* I, 176).

against it. Zeno states that destiny is not confined to some events which occur in the world. It extends to everything. Whatever happens in the evolution of the cosmos is settled by fate. This view is also accepted by Chrysippus and Posidonius. According to them, destiny is the unceasing cause of whatever exists. It is the reason according to which the world develops.[2]

At the end of his famous *Hymn to Zeus* Cleanthes declares that God governs the world with justice. Nothing that occurs in the world is unjust. Are the sufferings endured by so many unfairly imposed by an implacable divinity or a blind fate? Nothing could be farther from the truth. God is providence, and the work he realizes in the course of history bears the mark of his perfection. Man must ceaselessly praise the work of God and the universal law that governs the universe.[3] In his prayer Cleanthes does not ask that the course of history be changed or that some events be suppressed. He simply asks God to take away the darkness from his soul, so that he may recognize the divine law that governs the world. The prayer preserved in the *Enchiridion* of Epictetus is equally typical. The author implores Zeus and fate to lead him to the place assigned to him, so that he may follow without hesitation. Moreover, he is quite conscious of the fact that any opposition on his part would only result in making him guilty, for he is unable to change anything in the course of events.[4] The same notion is attributed to Cleanthes by a *Letter* of Seneca: *ducunt volentem fata, nolentem trahunt*.[5] It is useless to oppose destiny. No one can overcome its power.

Does not this rationalization of fate as worked out by the Stoics imply the denial of any kind of freedom or contingency? Does not this interpretation of the world and of history lead to total determinism, so that even the most intimate acts of the human soul are determined by the movements of the heavenly bodies? The Stoics constantly stress the importance of moral life. Man must live in conformity with nature or reason. There would be no point in formulating this rule if man cannot act differently. In that case, wisdom would be imprinted in his nature and his life would be

---

[2]Stobaeus, *Ecl.*, I, 79, 1 W. (*SVF* II, 913); Diog. Laërt., VII, 149 (Posidonius, vol. I, *The Fragments*, ed. L. Edelstein and I. G. Kidd, fr. 25 [*SVF* I, 175]).
[3]Stobaeus, *Ecl.*, I, 1, 12, p. 25, 3.
[4]Epictetus, *Man.*, c. 53 (*SVF* I, 527).
[5]Seneca, *Epist.* 107, 10 (*SVF* I, 527).

nothing but the unfolding of a film whose episodes had been settled in advance. This is certainly not the teaching of the Stoics. The great majority of men do not live in conformity with nature. Those whose lives are entirely in accord with reason are the exception. In the course of time the Stoics had to face many objections and criticisms. They constantly had to meet the argument that according to their position human freedom and responsibility were destroyed.

In connection with this I must mention Carneades, since his arguments against Stoic fatalism were frequently repeated by medieval authors. If everything is settled by fate, laws and punishments are meaningless. Human behavior is necessitated, just like everything else. There can be no question of virtue and vice, or of praise and blame. Will it still be appropriate to encourage people, or to reward them, or to express one's disapproval of them? In Carneades' view all such acts are quite useless if one admits the existence of destiny. In a word, all moral activity and even any endeavor of this kind are suppressed. The same holds for religious life. Piety and prayer become meaningless.[6] If one asks why Carneades himself firmly believes in man's freedom, there is only one reason, viz., common opinion or universal agreement. Carneades is convinced that all men agree on this point, and that this universal conviction is incorporated into the institutions and organizations of human society.[7]

At the beginning of the third century Alexander of Aphrodisias, one of the best-known commentators on Aristotle, devoted a special treatise to the question of fatalism.[8] This work was translated into Latin by William of Moerbeke in the second half of the thirteenth

---

[6]D. Amand, *Fatalisme et liberté dans l'antiquité grecque* (Louvain, 1945), pp. 62ff.

[7]Carneades agrees with Chrysippus that there is no movement without a cause. This viewpoint, however, does not imply that all events are produced by antecedent factors. Human decisions could not result from antecedent and external causes (Cicero, *De fato*, XI, 23). Hence movements of the will are not uncaused. They are in our power and obey us. The cause of these movements is the very nature of the will (Cicero, *De fato*, XI, 25). Movements of the will, instead of being subdued to some external rule, only develop according to their own rule; they are not heteronomous, but autonomous.

[8]Alexander Aphrodisiensis, *Scripta minora* (*Quaestiones, De Fato, De Mixtione*), ed. Ivo Bruns, Supplementum Aristotelicum, vol. II, pars 2 (Berlin, 1892).

century.⁹ In Cicero's *De Fato* Alexander is mentioned among those who defend fatalism.¹⁰ In fact Alexander does not hesitate to admit the existence of destiny because of the argument from universal agreement. Such consensus shows that this doctrine is the object of a natural, inborn, and anticipative knowledge.¹¹ Some events at least depend upon destiny. The question remains, however: precisely what does destiny mean and how far does it extend?¹²

In attempting to specify the kind of causality that is exercised by fate, Alexander eliminates material, formal, and final causality. Fate is an efficient cause, like a sculptor making a statue.¹³ Hence the question arises whether destiny is orientated towards an end. Alexander firmly believes that fate is directed towards an end. Since it is impossible to attribute to it human activity and moral life, he concludes that fate coincides with nature. As such it is the immanent principle of movements which occur within the world.¹⁴ Alexander also notes that what is caused by fate does not always and necessarily happen. It may be prevented by some external cause; and yet it generally happens, without being strictly necessitated.¹⁵ Therefore if, for instance, someone is ill, it is not useless to care for him and to seek the advice of a competent physician.¹⁶ Consequently, as an efficient cause destiny introduces into the world only limited neces-

---

⁹*Alexandre d'Aphrodise, De Fato ad imperatores. Version de Guillaume de Moerbeke, Édition critique avec Introduction et Index* by Pierre Thillet (Paris, 1963).

¹⁰Cicero, *De Fato*, XVII, 39.

¹¹In this context Alexander speaks of the κοινὴ τῶν ἀνθρώπων φύσις (*De Fato*, c. 2, p. 165, 16). This expression is important, for it indicates why such importance is attributed to anticipative knowledge. This knowledge belongs to the common nature of man, which could not possibly be orientated towards error (cf. *De Fato*, c. 12, p. 180, 24).

¹²*De Fato*, c. 2, p. 165, 23.

¹³Alexander does not hesitate to admit that fate is a cause, since there is (in his opinion) universal agreement on this subject. Everyone speaking about destiny believes it to be a cause of events occurring in the world (*De Fato*, c. 3, p. 166, 16).

¹⁴*De Fato*, c. 5, p. 168, 27; c. 6, p. 169, 19. The identification of nature and destiny does not correspond to the doctrine of Aristotle, but may be found in Stoic teaching. In Alexander's view, however, nature and reason do not coincide, whereas the Stoics maintain that nature is identical with universal reason.

¹⁵*De Fato*, c. 6, p. 170, 1.

¹⁶*De Fato*, c. 6, p. 171, 11ff.

sity. First of all, it does not govern human decisions and moral activity. Moreover, insofar as it governs the physical world, it most frequently produces the intended effect, but not always. As a result, there is no incompatibility between fatalism, contingency, and human freedom.[17] One of Plotinus's early treatises also deals with the problem of fatalism. Plotinus strongly rejects universal determinism, which holds that everything is settled by antecedent causes. According to this position not only external events but even the mind's activity would be necessitated by previous causal influences.[18] This finally implies that self-determination is only an empty word.[19] Plotinus does not agree with this theory. So long as the soul exists outside the body, it is totally free and master of itself; for it is not yet involved in the sequence of cosmic causes. When, however, the soul is joined to the body, it does not remain completely free; for it is then introduced into a whole, together with things in the world.[20] As a consequence, the soul's situation becomes ambiguous. Its activity is partly influenced by all kinds of causes which belong to the sensible world; but it also partly dominates and governs things according to its own decisions.[21] Plotinus emphasizes the point that not all human beings are equally free. The highest degree of freedom is reached when a person is governed by reason, being kept pure and not subjected to passions and emotions.[22] Thus everything that occurs has some

---

[17]Cf. Ps. Plutarch, *De Fato*, in *Plutarch's Moralia*, vol. VII, translated by Phillip H. De Lacy and B. Einarson, p. 306: "He [the author] considers fate to be a law which states that a certain consequent will follow upon a certain antecedent, but which does not thereby determine the antecedent." According to this view also fatalism is compatible with contingency and human freedom.
[18]*Enn.*, III, 1, 7, 9-15. Everything will be necessitated if all beings are in the power of fate. In that case, even our representations and the impulses they provoke will not escape from being determined. They will in their turn be inserted into the sequence of causes and effects.
[19]*Enn.*, III, 1, 7, 16: ὄνομα τε μόνον τὸ ἐφ' ἡμῖν ἔσται.
[20]*Enn.*, III, 1, 8, 10-12.
[21]*Enn.*, III, 1, 8, 12-14.
[22]*Enn.*, III, 1, 9, 9-16. In a sense each individual freely creates his own level of freedom. If some individuals reach a higher degree of freedom than others, it is as a result of their previous behavior, and not because a particular level of free choice has been allotted to them from the beginning of their life.

cause. It is partly produced by the soul and partly by external causes. As we have already noted in Alexander, so too in Plotinus destiny's domination is far from universal. It does not destroy human freedom, which itself reaches a higher level insofar as the mind liberates itself from external pressures to a greater degree. Around the end of the fourth century Nemesius, Bishop of Emesa in Syria, composed his famous *De natura hominis*. This work was very influential. It was translated into Armenian, Georgian, and Arabic. During the Middle Ages it was twice translated into Latin, first by Alfanus of Salerno and later by Burgundio of Pisa. During the Renaissance it was translated into Latin three more times.[23] An important section in this treatise is devoted to the question of fate, providence, and freedom. This subject was obviously controversial. Dating back to the same period is a work by Gregory of Nyssa entitled *Contra fatum*, which is connected with a public debate in Constantinople between Gregory and a pagan philosopher, probably a follower of the Stoics.[24]

In his exposition Nemesius distinguishes five different interpretations of destiny. The most radical form of fatalism declares that whatever occurs is determined and necessitated by the movements of the heavenly bodies.[25] Nemesius opposes this view since it is contrary to common opinions (κοιναῖς ἐννοίαις).[26] Moreover, if one were to accept this kind of determinism, all political organization would become useless. Praise and blame would lose their meaning. Every prayer would be deprived of value. Such a theory implies the rejection of divine providence and of all forms of religion. In sum it entails the denial of any contingency or freedom. Finally, who could be guilty of wrongdoing, of injustice, adultery or murder? According to radical fatalism all such acts would have to be imputed to the heavenly bodies and ultimately to God himself. How could

---

[23]*Némésius d'Emèse, De natura hominis. Traduction de Burgundio de Pise, édition critique avec une Introduction sur l'anthropologie de Némésius*, by G. Verbeke and J.R. Moncho (Leiden, 1975), pp. lxxxvi-c.

[24]*Contra Fatum*, PG 45, 169: According to Gregory fate is to be identified with the free choice of each individual. In other words, fate is not a power compelling us from without. It coincides with our autonomous decision.

[25]*De natura hominis*, XXXIV, p. 133, 59.

[26]*De natura hominis*, XXXIV, p. 133, 59-60.

one avoid accusing the divine Creator of the most horrible crimes?[27] All of these criticisms of this extreme fatalism belong to the tradition that comes from Carneades. The same objections occur in almost identical fashion in the writings of many pagan and Christian authors.[28] Even Aquinas briefly expounds these arguments in his study of human freedom.[29]

A second form of fatalism, more moderate than the first, is associated with two Stoic philosophers, Chrysippus and Philopator.[30] According to these writers, destiny and human freedom are not incompatible. Every being is endowed with some characteristic properties that spring from destiny. Thus it belongs to water to be cold, to plants to produce their specific fruits, to stones to fall, and to flames to rise. The same holds for living beings. It rests with them alone to consent to objects they perceive and to move by themselves. Beings of this kind tend to certain objects, provided there is no external obstacle and provided they are not prevented from doing this by the interference of another fate.[31]

According to Nemesius, there is little difference between this theory and radical fatalism. In fact everything is settled by destiny. The impulse itself stems from destiny, and the result of the act— to attain the goal pursued—may always be thwarted by destiny. Freedom of action is totally suppressed. That even the impulse is necessitated by fate is due to the fact that the same causes always produce the same effects. There will be no difference between human conduct and animal behavior. Just as the activity of an animal necessarily flows from fate, so all components of a human decision, even judgment and consent, are fixed by the same blind power. What can the result be, but that there is no place for free activity? If, according to Stoic teaching, the history of the world is an unbreakable sequence of causes and effects, it will hardly be possible to

---

[27]*De natura hominis*, XXXIV, p. 133, 60–77.
[28]D. Amand, *Fatalisme et liberté dans l'antiquité grecque*, pp. 41–68.
[29]*Summa Theologiae*, I, q. 83, a. 1.
[30]The available information about Philopator is rather meager. He probably lived in the second century A.D. and wrote a treatise entitled *De Fato* (Περὶ εἱμαρμένης), in which he tried to support the view of Chrysippus and to safeguard human freedom without abandoning the notion of destiny (M. Pohlenz, *Die Stoa*, I, p. 345; II, p. 147).
[31]*De natura hominis*, XXXIV, pp. 133, 78–134, 96.

introduce autonomous initiative into this unfolding process. Human activity will also be thrown into this machinery.[32]

The fourth theory concerning fate is ascribed by Nemesius to "the wisest among the Greeks." These again are Stoics.[33] According to these philosophers, choice itself depends upon our free initiative, whereas the result of human activity is regulated by destiny. As a matter of fact, this theory is in accord with Stoic philosophy and fits in with other parts of that system. The Stoics do not extend the field of free initiative to external events, to the transformation of the sensible world. It is rather confined to the realm of internal decisions—the attitude adopted by man towards fortunate and unfortunate events. Man can accept the course of history or oppose it; but he is unable to introduce any change into it because it depends entirely upon divine Reason. Nemesius agrees to some extent with this theory insofar as it recognizes the freedom of human activity. He also accepts the conclusion that the results of decisions are not totally within man's power.[34] And yet he disagrees with the Stoics when they state that the outcome of our activity depends on fate. In his opinion, this outcome is rather in the hands of divine providence.[35]

According to Nemesius there is considerable difference between fate and providence. Whereas destiny is an invariable chain of causes and effects, providence supplies for everyone that which is profitable and beneficial.[36] If one accepts the Stoic viewpoint, one cannot explain why some individuals suffer from mental illness and are unable to make free decisions. Since this illness itself is caused by destiny, the result will be that no one is the principle of decision

---

[32]*De natura hominis*, XXXIV, pp. 134, 86–135, 11.
[33]*De natura hominis*, XXXVI, p. 137, 60–61.
[34]*De natura hominis*, XXXVI, p. 137, 62–63.
[35]Nemesius objects against the Stoic doctrine that it implies that destiny is imperfect, since human decision escapes from its domination. In a sense destiny is subject to man, since it is influenced by the decisions which an individual makes (*De natura hominis*, XXXVI, p. 137, 64–69).
[36]Nemesius refers to the Stoic definition of fate (*De natura hominis*, XXXVII, p. 178, 65–69; Aëtius, *Plac.*, I, 28, 4 [Diels 324, 1–3; *SVF* II, 917, p. 265, 36–37]). As far as the sequence of external events is concerned, whatever occurs is linked to its cause from which it inevitably results. There is no contingency. The present situation of the world is a necessary effect of the past. There is only one path along which divine Reason leads world history.

Fatalism and Freedom 79

for himself. Even the capacity to choose will flow from destiny.³⁷ This theory ultimately leads to universal determinism, which it attempts to avoid. Nemesius's doctrine was later taken up again by John Damascene who, however, formulates it more accurately. According to John, God knows our free decisions beforehand without predetermining them.³⁸ According to Nemesius, man's free choices do not fall under divine providence. They are located outside its concern.³⁹

On the whole, Nemesius's teaching on destiny is a positive contribution to the interpretation of Christianity in that he emphasizes both the autonomy of human behavior and the sovereign freedom of God. One of the central themes of his teaching is his view that God cannot be subordinated to any form of constraint. God is supremely free. This is one of the most important innovations with respect to astrology and other fatalistic doctrines which were widespread during the Hellenistic period. It also marks progress as regards Stoicism itself. This system had rationalized destiny by identifying it with the divine Logos that governs the course of history. This Reason is materialized in identical fashion in the succeeding periods of the world's development. Nemesius even improves upon Plotinus, who holds that the process of emanation from the One is both necessary and spontaneous. It belongs to the nature of the Good to communicate its perfection and consequently to give rise to other beings that may profit from its fullness. According to Nemesius, God dominates all necessity and all constraint. He is the free and creative source of whatever exists.

There is, however, an important qualification in Nemesius's theory. Divine providence is restricted to those things which do not depend on our free initiative. What proceeds from our choice is outside its scope. The reason for this interpretation may easily be discerned. A free decision belongs entirely to man. In fact, Nemesius

---

³⁷*De natura hominis*, XXXVI, p. 138, 78–84.
³⁸Joannes Damascenus, *De fide orthodoxa*, ed. Buytaert, c. 44, p. 161: Oportet noscere quod omnia quidem praenoscit Deus, non omnia autem praedeterminat. Praenoscit enim et quae in nobis, non praedeterminat autem ea. Non enim vult malitiam fieri, neque compellit virtutem.
³⁹*De natura hominis*, XLII, p. 161, 21: providentia vero eorum quae non sunt in nobis; *ibid.*, p. 169, 33; Joannes Damascenus, *op. cit.*, c. 43, p. 157: Omnia autem dico quae non in nobis; quae enim in nobis, non providentiae sunt, sed nostri liberi arbitrii.

is coping with the very difficult question of divine creative causality and human freedom. Wanting to preserve human freedom at any price, he found himself unable to offer any other solution. He could only remove human choice from divine providence. Being endowed with reason, man is capable of free choice; for a rational being can deliberate. Not being determined by surrounding circumstances, man has the ability to adopt a proper perspective and to consider all the elements of a given situation.[40] The power of deliberation would be completely useless if man were unable to act according to his own intuition and choice.[41] The knowledge in question is obviously not speculative. It is a practical intuition telling us how to behave in a particular situation.[42] Human life is always changing. It is never invariably settled in a given condition. It is integrated within the world evolution of which it is a part. This changeable character of man follows from the basic character of his being. Life begins at a particular moment and man's structure involves a material principle.[43] Consequently, human freedom is marked by the same mutability. It can develop in one way or another. God is in no way the author of man's evildoing. Each individual is responsible for his own behavior. Hence the question arises whether human freedom itself is evil. Nemesius firmly denies this. If a man behaves badly, it is not because he has the power of choice but because his dispositions, acquired by his freely decided actions, are themselves evil. The fact that some individuals wrongly use their power of choice is no argument for concluding that human freedom is evil in itself.[44]

At about this same period Calcidius, also a Christian, deals with the problem of fatalism in his Commentary on the *Timaeus* of

---

[40]*De natura hominis*, XXXI, p. 125, 92-94; Arist., *Eth. Nic.*, III, 3, 1111a22-24.
[41]*De natura hominis*, XL, pp. 149, 23-150, 48. The same argument was put forward by Alexander of Aphrodisias in his *De Fato* (cf. G. Verbeke, "Aristotélisme et Stoïcisme dans le *De fato* d'Alexandre d'Aphrodisias," p. 87).
[42]*De natura hominis*, XL, pp. 149, 37-151, 41.
[43]*De natura hominis*, XL, p. 150, 48-51.
[44]Should wrong actions be attributed to man's faculties? Not according to Nemesius. They do not result from our faculties, but from our dispositions and choices, i.e., from our moral attitude (*De natura hominis*, XL, p. 151, 83: non enim in virtutibus sunt malitiae, sed in habitibus; habitus autem secundum electionem sunt; p. 152, 94: non sunt igitur virtutum malitiae, sed habituum et electionis).

Plato. This commentary is extensive and is also one of the main sources through which Plato's philosophy, especially his cosmology, was made known to the Middle Ages.[45] The fact that Calcidius devotes so many pages to the problem of destiny shows that this issue was still controversial even among Christians. Had not Origen written in his *De principiis* that many Christians favored fatalism? Calcidius too, though a Christian, does not reject this doctrine out of hand. He rather tries to make it compatible with Christian teaching on divine providence and human freedom.[46] Already from the beginning of his exposition, while referring to Plato, he emphasizes the priority of providence and fate's subordination to it.[47] Such an interpretation implies an important qualification of the traditional view as well as of Stoic teaching on destiny. In developing this view, Calcidius states that the highest principle which governs and dominates everything is God. He is the highest good, the supreme perfection, and everything else strives toward him.[48] Then follows providence, which coincides with intellect (νοῦς according to the Greeks). This principle is always orientated towards the highest good and receives its perfection from this source. It is the eternal mind of God which extends its wise protection over all that exists.[49] Calcidius puts destiny on a third level. Destiny is the divine law promulgated for the appropriate government of all things.[50] The world-soul, which he calls the second intellect, obeys this divine law through which everything is directed in accord with its nature.[51] This subordination of fate to the highest divine principle and to providence is an important adaptation of fatalism to Christian belief. On the other hand, Calcidius apparently takes from Neoplatonism his inspiration for the three principal hypostases—the One, the Intellect, and universal Soul.

[45]*Timaeus a Calcidio translatus commentarioque instructus*, ed. J.H. Waszink, Plato Latinus, vol. IV, 2nd ed. (London-Leiden, 1975).
[46]*Timaeus*, Praefatio, p. xi.
[47]*Timaeus*, c. 143, p. 181: Igitur iuxta Platonem praecedit providentia, sequitur fatum.
[48]*Timaeus*, c. 176, p. 204.
[49]*Timaeus*, c. 176, pp. 204–5.
[50]*Timaeus*, c. 177, p. 206: Sequitur hanc providentiam fatum, lex divina promulgata intelligentiae sapienti modulamine ad rerum omnium gubernationem.
[51]*Timaeus*, c. 177, p. 206.

Calcidius also tries to preserve human freedom without abandoning fatalism. He is well aware of the many objections and difficulties. First of all, there is the problem of divine foreknowledge. If God knows everything, not only the past and the present but also the future, not only external events but even our most secret thoughts and desires, everything must have been settled from the very beginning. This will mean that everything depends on fate—not only what actually occurs, but also the conditions and circumstances within which it happens.[52] Those writers who defend universal fatalism also have recourse to divination. The future could not be foretold if it had not been settled and determined in advance.[53] Calcidius agrees that God knows everything; but he knows each thing according to its nature—what is necessary as necessary, what is changeable and contingent as changeable and contingent.[54] Regarding divination, Calcidius introduces some qualifications. Divination is clearly possible in the field of necessary events because they inevitably proceed from their causes. Where contingent events are concerned, however, these can be known only insofar as their outcome is already given. Otherwise, any prediction concerning the future could only be uncertain.[55] When human activity is involved, prediction formulated hypothetically may be regarded as a kind of advice. The prediction states that a particular event will happen if man behaves in such or such a way.[56] In connection with fatalism, Calcidius also rejects the view that evil flows from the heavenly bodies which constantly influence all that occurs in the world.[57] Finally, he rejects the doctrine that everything, including human behavior, is controlled by an immanent reason which regulates all events through an unbreakable chain of causes.[58] At the end of his exposi-

---

[52] *Timaeus*, c. 160, p. 194.
[53] *Timaeus*, c. 161, p. 194.
[54] *Timaeus*, c. 162, p. 195: Quod deus sciat quidem omnia sed unumquidque pro natura sua ipsorum sciat: necessitati quidem subiugatum, ut necessitati obnoxium, anceps vero, ut quod ea sit natura praeditum, cui consilium viam pandat; neque enim ita scit ambigui naturam deus, ut quod certum et necessitate constrictum (sic enim falletur et nesciet) sed ita, ut pro natura sua vere dubium sciat.
[55] *Timaeus*, c. 169, p. 199; c. 185, p. 211.
[56] *Timaeus*, cc. 170–71, pp. 200–201.
[57] *Timaeus*, c. 174, p. 202.
[58] *Timaeus*, c. 175, p. 203.

tion Calcidius comments that we must admit both human freedom and fate. Those who deny the existence of destiny are mistaken; but those who reject human freedom are equally mistaken.[59] Calcidius's view, that of a Christian at the beginning of the fifth century, is obviously an interesting attempt to reconcile fatalism and human freedom.

Proclus was not a Christian. During the second half of the fifth century he was head of the School of Philosophy at Athens, and wrote a penetrating treatise concerning fatalism and freedom. This work was translated into Latin in the thirteenth century by William of Moerbeke under the title *De providentia et fato et eo quod in nobis*.[60] This treatise is addressed to Theodorus who maintains that providence alone is free. Human freedom is an empty phrase and refers to nothing.[61] In his reply Proclus strongly opposes this position, but without denying the existence of fate. According to him, destiny coincides with nature and is the origin of the connections which exist among things.[62] Destiny exercises its influence and activity over changeable and corporeal things. In other words, fate's causality is confined to the physical world.[63] In addition, fate is subordinated to providence. While providence is by itself a god, fate is something divine but not a god. In Proclus's terminology, destiny is an image of providence.[64] It is on a lower level and yet is to some

[59]*Timaeus*, c. 190, p. 214: Namque fato quaedam agi verum est, et quod quaedam in nostra potestate sint, hoc quoque verum esse monstratum est. Quae qui omnia fato fieri dicunt, merito reprehenduntur ab his qui probant esse aliquid in nostra potestate, demum qui omnia in nostra potestate constituunt nec quicquam fato relinquunt, falli deteguntur; quis enim ignoret esse aliquid in fato et extra nostrum ius? Sola igitur vera illa ratio est fixaque et stabilis sententia, quae docet quaedam fato fieri, alia porro ex hominum arbitrio et voluntate proficisci.

[60]*Procli Diadochi Tria Opuscula, latine Guilelmo de Moerbeka vertente, et graece ex Isaacii Sebastocratoris aliorumque scriptis collecta*, ed. H. Boese (Berlin, 1960); *De providentia et fato et eo quod in nobis*, pp. 109-71.

[61]*De providentia*, c. 2, p. 110: humane autem anime divulgatum autexusion nomen solum esse et ut vere nichil, ordinata qua in mundo et serviente aliorum actionibus et existente parte mundialis operis.

[62]*De providentia*, c. 11, p. 118: necesse utique naturam causam esse connexorum et in hac querere vocatum fatum.

[63]*De providentia*, c. 10, p. 116.

[64]*De providentia*, c. 14, p. 122: dependet enim (scil. fatum) a providentia et velut ymago est illius.

extent similar to providence. It extends the governance of providence into the physical world.

What then of human freedom? According to Proclus, human soul is beyond destiny by reason of its nature, but may be subordinated to it in its activity.[65] The degree of freedom is not the same in each individual. Some are freer than others because of their own moral conduct. If a man behaves badly, if his soul clings to the senses and to material desires, he becomes more and more corporeal and consequently more and more subject to the control of fate.[66] Human soul is really free only insofar as it participates in moral virtue. Only a virtuous man is fully free, whereas an immoral individual lives in a permanent condition of slavery. He is the slave of his passions and emotions.[67] Rational soul finds itself in an ambiguous situation. Being at once mind and sense, it is constantly unstable and capable of moving in either direction. It may move upward towards the intellect, or downward towards the senses.[68] The level of moral freedom and behavior ultimately depends upon the soul itself. The condition of the soul depends upon its own decisions and choices. Not everything, of course, depends upon our choices. Life is a mixture of things which are freely decided by ourselves and others which do not proceed from our choices.[69]

Proclus also deals with the difficult question of divine foreknowledge and explicitly refers to Stoic determinism.[70] He firmly maintains that the gods know in advance whatever happens, including human decisions. This knowledge, however, does not imply determinism, since it is divine and atemporal, or beyond time. In other words, such knowledge does not depend upon the fact that man has

---

[65] *De providentia*, c. 20, p. 128.
[66] *De providentia*, c. 21, p. 130: per hoc enim corporeizamur, et corporati ex necessitate a fato ducimur.
[67] *De providentia*, c. 24, p. 132: omnis igitur anima secundum quod virtute participat, et eo quod est liberum esse; c. 25, p. 136.
[68] *De providentia*, c. 44, p. 154: Media enim rationalis anima intellectus et sensus ens, fertur quidem ad ambo propter instabilem electionis inclinationem.
[69] *De providentia*, c. 61, p. 167: propter quod commixta vita nostra ex hiis que non in nobis et ex hiis que in nobis.
[70] *De providentia*, c. 63, p. 168: alii autem determinatam cognitionem attribuentes deo, admiserunt necessitatem in omnibus que fiunt: Peripateticorum et Stoicorum heresum sunt hec dogmata.

already made a particular decision. It is beyond the gradual process of time and is directly related to the divine perfection.[71] According to Proclus, human freedom must be preserved at any price. Otherwise, philosophy becomes quite useless.[72] In Calcidius and in Proclus the essential feature of Stoic fatalism has been preserved. Destiny is no longer a blind and irrational power. It has a definite function in the divine governance of the world.

Boethius also had to come to terms with the problem of fatalism and freedom. In his case this problem was not only theoretical, but was closely associated with the personal misfortune he was forced to undergo at the end of his life. In his *De consolatione Philosophiae* he tries to draw a clear distinction between providence and fate.[73] He subordinates the latter to the former; destiny is at a lower level than providence. While destiny is a moving sequence of causes, providence is an unchangeable unity and simplicity.[74] This relationship may be compared to that between reasoning and intellectual intuition, between coming to be and being, between time and eternity, or between a circle and its center.[75] According to Boethius, providence coincides with the divine mind. Since providence is placed in the highest principle of all things, it governs all that exists. Fate is the harmonious disposition present in moving reality—a disposition by means of which everything is in its proper place.[76] While providence embraces all beings equally, fate puts particular things into movement by assigning to them a place, a shape, and a time. This unfolding in time, when viewed in its unity by the divine mind, is providence; but when it is diffused and extended through

---

[71]*De providentia*, c. 65, p. 170: Quare et cognoscunt dii divine et incorporaliter que in nobis et nos operamur ut apti nati sumus; et quodcumque eligimus precognitum est apud ipsos, non propter in nobis terminum, sed propter eum qui apud ipsos.
[72]*De providentia*, c. 66, p. 170.
[73]*Anicii Manlii Severini Boethii Philosophiae consolatio*, ed. L. Bieler (Turnhout, 1957).
[74]*De consolatione*, IV, 6, 13: illud certe manifestum est immobilem simplicemque gerendarum formam rerum esse prouidentiam, fatum uero eorum, quae divina simplicitas gerenda disposuit, mobilem nexum atque ordinem temporalem.
[75]*De consolatione*, IV, 6, 17.
[76]*De consolatione*, IV, 6, 9: nam prouidentia est ipsa illa diuina ratio in summo omnium principe constituta, quae cuncta disponit, fatum vero inhaerens rebus mobilibus dispositio, per quam prouidentia suis quaeque nectit ordinibus.

the various instants of time, it coincides with fate.[77] As a consequence, whatever is subject to fate is also subject to providence; but there are things which depend on providence without their being subordinated to the causal chain of fate.[78]

At the same time, Boethius defends human freedom. Being endowed with reason, man must be free; for he has the capacity to judge. Hence he can by himself distinguish between objects which are to be pursued and those which are to be avoided.[79] And yet, Boethius immediately adds that not everyone is equally free. Like Proclus, Boethius holds that one's degree of freedom is closely connected with the level of one's moral life. If an individual is dominated by various kinds of vicious attitudes, he may even lose his capacity to think and become a slave to his own passions.[80] Finally, Boethius raises the question whether human freedom is compatible with God's foreknowledge. His reply to this question corresponds in large measure to that of Proclus. God's knowledge even of contingent future events is not uncertain. This certainty does not depend on the nature of the object known but on that of the knowing subject.[81] This divine knowing subject can grasp in a single and undivided view things that are multiple and immersed in the flow of time.[82] This divine knowledge is not necessitating. Man remains free, though all his decisions and acts are known beforehand by the all-embracing knowledge of God.[83]

---

[77]*De consolatione*, IV, 6, 10: Prouidentia namque cuncta pariter quamuis diuersa quamuis infinita complectitur, fatum uero singula digerit in motum locis, formis ac temporibus distributa, ut haec temporalis ordinis explicatio in diuinae mentis adunata prospectum prouidentia sit, eadem uero adunatio digesta atque explicata temporibus fatum uocetur.

[78]*De consolatione*, IV, 6, 14.

[79]*De consolatione*, V, 2, 3–4.

[80]*De consolatione*, V, 2, 9: extrema uero est seruitus cum uitiis deditae rationis propriae possessione ceciderunt.

[81]*De consolatione*, V, 4, 24: Cuius erroris causa est quod omnia quae quisque nouit ex ipsorum tantum ui atque natura cognosci aestimat quae sciuntur. Quod totum contra est: omne enim quod cognoscitur non secundum sui uim sed secundum cognoscentium potius comprehenditur facultatem.

[82]*De consolatione*, V, 5, 12.

[83]*De consolatione*, V, 4, 20: Nam sicut scientia praesentium rerum nihil his quae fiunt ita praescientia futurorum nihil his quae uentura sunt necessitatis importat. I was wondering whether I should deal at this stage with the ninth-century debate on predestination. It was surely a major controversy

Boethius's view was adopted by outstanding representatives of medieval thought such as Albert the Great, Ulrich of Strasburg, and John Duns Scotus. The ancient mythological notion of fate had been thoroughly transformed. The Stoics had rationalized it. The Neoplatonists subordinated destiny to divine providence and made it compatible with human freedom. Thus the doctrine of fatalism could now be integrated into the great theological syntheses of the thirteenth century. In dealing with the notions of chance and fortune, Albert fully recognizes the instability of the material world. Sensible reality is constantly becoming and changing. Sensible things need a bond that links them together, a rule that governs them. This rule is thought to be *fatum*, which the Greeks call εἱμαρμένη. Albert's main concern apparently is to account for the coherence and appropriate disposition of the universe.[84] Chance is an undetermined cause, introduced in order to account for phenomena which escape from the essential finality of the world. Chance's action is unpredictable and is not open to scientific investigation. Given this, how is one to safeguard the harmonious unfolding of history? In reply, Albert appeals to the notion of destiny. This he defines as a sequence of causes governed by the providence of the First Principle.

In this context Albert quotes the *De natura deorum of Hermes Trismegistos*,[85] as well as Apuleius (known mainly through the

---

in which many authors were involved, among others John Scotus Eriugena. I finally decided not to treat it. I realize that predestination is connected with the topic of necessity and freedom, but was unable to discover a sufficiently clear link between Stoic philosophy and predestination.

[84]*B. Alberti Magni Opera omnia*, ed. A. Borgnet, 38 vols. (Vives edition, Paris, 1890). The Commentary on Aristotle's *Physics*, in which Albert deals with the question of fate, is included in vol. III, pp. 1–632; cf. p. 155 (II, 2, 20): Propter quod fatum superfluum est eis, sicut vinculum continens ea et sicut regula regens. Among the works attributed to Thomas Aquinas and printed in the Vives edition (*Opera omnia* [Paris, 1875], vol. XXVII, opusculum XXIV, pp. 454–64), there is a writing entitled: *De Fato secundum Albertum*; this treatise has been proved to belong to Albert and has therefore been put in the critical edition of Albert's works (*Opera omnia*, XVII, P. Simon ed. [Münster i.W., 1975]). Cf. L. Thorndike, *A History of Magic and Experimental Science during the First Thirteen Centuries of our Era*, 3rd. ed. (New York, 1943), vol. II, pp. 612–15; M. Grabmann, *Die Werke des hl. Thomas von Aquin* (Münster i.W., 1949), p. 399.

[85]*Opera omnia*, III, p. 153 (II, 2, 19).

Metamorphoses), the *De mundo*, *De deo Socratis*, and *De Platone et eius dogmate*.[86] In addition he refers to the astronomer Firmitius (Julius Firmicius Maternus), an astrologer from the fourth century A.D. who authored a work entitled *Matheseos libri VIII*, where he tries to show that astrology is compatible with human freedom.[87] Albert also cites Ptolemy, the well-known astronomer of the second century A.D., whose *Almagest* had first been translated into Arabic in the ninth century and later into Latin in the twelfth century by Gerard of Cremona.[88] Among those quoted by Albert I should also mention Seneca, who in many writings adopts the Stoic teaching on fate, and Boethius, who is the main source for Albert's teaching on this topic both in his Commentary on the *Physics* and in his *Summa Theologiae*.

According to Albert, it is quite impossible for one to deny destiny as it has been defined here. One can hardly reject the regular concatenation of causes and effects which guarantees that each cause produces a specific effect. Since this sequence is undeniable and since it coincides with destiny, one cannot deny the existence of destiny.[89] Still, fate does not govern the course of history as a sovereign master. Fate itself is subject to divine providence. Providence grasps everything in an intemporal and eternal knowing. Since it is the creative cause, it is at the origin of all that exists, including the development of the world and the course of history.[90]

---

[86]In the first book of his *De Platone et eius dogmate* (I, 12, p. 95, 17, ed. P. Thomas) the author writes about Plato: Quare nec omnia ad fati sortem arbitratur esse referenda. Ita enim definit: providentiam esse divinam sententiam conservatricem prosperitatis eius, cuius causa tale suscipit officium; divinam legem esse fatum, per quod inevitabiles cogitationes dei atque incepta complentur. Unde si quid providentia geritur, id agitur etiam fato, et quod fato terminatur, providentia debet inceptum videri.

[87]Firmicius Maternus, *Mathesis*, libri I–IV, ed.W. Kroll and F. Skutsch (Stuttgart, 1963); libri V–VIII, ed. W. Kroll, F. Skutsch, and K. Ziegler (Stuttgart, 1968); cf. I, 6.

[88]In his *Summa Theologiae*, I, 17, q. 68, 1 (*Opera omnia*, XXXI, p. 616) Albert maintains that the influence of the heavenly bodies is not necessitating. In this context he quotes Ptolemy: Ut dicit Ptolemaeus in *Centilogio*. Dicit enim quod "sapiens homo dominatur astris." The text of the Μεγάλη Σύνταξις has been edited by J.L. Heiberg (Teubner 1898 and 1903).

[89]*Opera omnia*, III, p. 154 (II, 2, 19); *Summa Theologiae*, I, 17, q. 68, 3 (*Opera omnia*, XXXI, p. 704).

[90]*Summa Theologiae*, I, 17, q. 68, 1 (*Opera omnia*, XXXI, p. 695): Unde

Fatalism and Freedom   89

But why postulate this intermediary power—destiny? Can providence not directly govern all created beings? Albert believes that it cannot because of the simplicity and intemporal nature of God. The well-ordered disposition of events introduced by fate proceeds from the simplicity and eternity of providence. God disposes everything by his providence and in accord with it in simple and immutable fashion. Thanks to destiny and through its mediation he directs, arranges, and governs these same things in temporal and diverse fashion. This corresponds to Boethius's position.[91] Taking his inspiration from Neoplatonism, Albert regards fate as an indispensable intermediary which is required to bridge the distance between the simplicity of divine knowing and willing and the multiplicity, temporality, and becoming of the material world.[92] He states this explicitly. God's science is the ultimate cause of whatever exists. Is it also the direct and immediate cause of things? Not according to Albert. Through the mediation of universal causes, God's science produces particular ones; and with the help of particular causes it produces whatever occurs in the world whether this is due to nature or to man's free activity.[93]

If everything is controlled by destiny, does not this imply that everything is necessitated? Albert replies first of all that not everything is controlled by destiny. All things are subject to divine providence, but not all that is subject to providence is governed by fate. The movement of heavenly bodies does not depend upon fate. Fate first realizes itself in the movement of the stars. It expresses itself in

---

providentia et fatum differunt ut exemplar et exemplatum, et sicut causa influens et forma influxa. Propter quod etiam Hermes Trismegistus et Plato mundum ab hoc exemplari egressum describunt, quasi secundum Deum a Deo deorum formatum. Et hoc modo ponere fatum nihil est inconveniens.

[91]*Opera omnia*, III, p. 153 (II, 2, 19). Albert was quite aware of the difficulty he had to face in introducing fate. In creating the world God does not need any intermediary or instrumental cause. Why does he need one in order to govern the cosmos? Albert replies that the situation is not the same in the two cases. Creation does not presuppose anything, whereas government always implies beings made "able to be governed" (*gubernabile*) (*Summa Theologiae*, I, 17, q. 68, 2; *Opera omnia*, III, p. 700).

[92]*Summa Theologiae*, I, 17, q. 68, 2 (*Opera omnia*, III, p. 700). In referring to fate Albert writes: Sic enim est inhaerens dispositio mobilibus causis et causatis, per quam sicut instrumentum providentia quaeque suis nectit ordinibus.

[93]*Opera omnia*, III, p. 153 (II, 2, 19).

the regular movements of the heavenly bodies. Destiny's action extends to changing realities which need a bond to prevent them from being totally dissolved. Consequently, destiny's influence extends to the field of coming to be and passing away.[94]

Will this result in universal determinism? Not according to Albert. He acknowledges that fate is necessary to some degree (*quodammodo necessarium*), but does not admit that it introduces necessity into things. He even confesses his willingness to drop his doctrine on destiny if this is regarded as an unbreakable law which proceeds from the movement of the heavenly bodies and imposes unchangeable behavior on lower beings.[95] According to Albert, the action of heavenly bodies is not coercive, not even on purely corporeal things. He refers to Ptolemy who writes that the action of heavenly bodies is unchanging, but that participation in this action by lower bodies is not unchanging. The influence of heavenly bodies is received in the same fashion by all things. It is participated in *per accidens* in accord with the various beings to which it extends.[96] Consequently, destiny as understood by Albert is not only compatible with human freedom; it does not even exclude chance and fortune. In his Commentary on the *Peri Hermeneias*, Albert categorically defends the contingency of human behavior as well as of natural phenomena. There are things which are not always in act either in themselves or in their causes. Of two contradictory alterna-

---

[94]*Opera omnia*, III, p. 155 (II, 2, 20); *Summa Theologiae*, I, 17, q. 68, 3 (*Opera omnia*, XXXI, p. 703); cf. Boethius, *De consolatione*, IV, 6, 14–15. In the synthesis which has been composed of Scotus's teaching a whole question (*quaestio* 116) is directed to the notion of fate. One of the problems raised is whether everything is subject to fate. The answer is negative. What is immediately created by God does not depend upon fate as far as its existence is concerned. Nor is rational soul subject to destiny since it is immaterial (*Joannis Duns Scoti Summa Theologica, ex universis operibus eius concinnata* per Hieronymum de Montefortino, Vol. I, 3 [Rome, 1901]). Consequently not everything that depends on providence depends on fate.

[95]*Opera omnia*, III, p. 154 (II, 2, 19): Verumtamen infra ostendemus, quod licet fatum sit quodammodo necessarium, non tamen imponit necessitatem rebus; et si in hoc sensu negatur fatum esse, prout dicit legem ex superiorum motu provenientem, inferiora ad eventus immobiles obligantem, etiam ego sum de negantibus fatum (cf. *Summa Theologiae*, I, 17, q. 68, 2; *Opera omnia*, XXXI, p. 701).

[96]*Opera omnia*, III, p. 156 (II, 2, 20); *Summa Theologiae*, I, 17, q. 67, 1 (*Opera omnia*, XXXI, p. 697).

tives concerning a future event, neither is true in definitive fashion. The disjunctive proposition is necessarily true, but neither of the alternatives is true beforehand.[97]

Thomas Aquinas is not satisfied with this teaching on destiny or on the role assigned to fate in the government of the world. He repeatedly faces this question and his attitude remains fundamentally the same.[98] In his Commentary on the *Peri Hermeneias* he carefully examines the notion of fate. There he distinguishes three different interpretations of this concept. First of all, there is the Stoic position. Fate is regarded as an unbreakable concatenation of causes and effects. Everything that happens in the world must be traced back to a cause. When that cause is given, the effect inevitably follows.[99] In some cases, one single cause will not be sufficient to produce the effect; but then the concurrence of various causes will have the same result as one single sufficient cause. Hence everything that happens, being the consequence of antecedent factors, happens necessarily.[100]

This interpretation does indeed correspond to the Stoic view of the cosmos as a living organism in which all parts are connected with one another. It also squares with the Stoic teaching concerning seminal reasons. In the history of the cosmos nothing is entirely new and original. Everything is in a way present from the very beginning —the succession of events being the unfolding of an initial seed. Aquinas strongly rejects this view which would exclude every kind of contingency. According to him, not all that occurs has its proper cause. Whatever happens accidentally (*per accidens*) does not have its own cause, because it does not exist by itself. It can only exist

---

[97]*Opera omnia*, I, p. 422 (I, 5, 6).
[98]*Summa contra Gentiles*, III, 93; *Comp. Theol.*, c. 138; *Summa Theologiae*, I, q. 116; *Quodl.* XII, q. 4; *In Matth.*, c. 2; *In Peri Hermeneias*, I, 14; *In Metaph.*, VI, 3.
[99]*In Aristotelis libros Peri Hermeneias et Posteriorum Analyticorum expositio*, ed. R.M. Spiazzi (Marietti), I, 14, n. 185: Quorum Stoici posuerunt fatum in quadam serie, seu connexione causarum, supponentes quod omne quod in hoc mundo accidit habet causam; causa autem posita, necesse est effectum poni.
[100]*In Peri Hermeneias*, I, 14, n. 185: Et si una causa per se non sufficit, multae causae ad hoc concurrentes accipiunt rationem unius causae sufficientis; et ita concludunt quod omnia ex necessitate eveniunt.

insofar as it is connected with something else, a substance.[101] Does Aquinas mean that whatever is accidental has no causal connection with anything antecedent? Not at all. There must be correspondence between cause and effect. If the effect is accidental, the cause belongs to the same level—a level which is very low on the ontological scale.[102] Accidents do not exist in the proper sense; they rather belong to the realm of nonbeing since they do not exist in themselves. As regards the teaching of the Stoics, it should be noted that not everything has its proper cause whereby it is produced. According to them, this does not apply to that which is accidental.

Does a cause necessarily imply its effect? According to Thomas a cause may be prevented from producing its effect, even if the cause is a sufficient one.[103] It may happen that owing to the action of some other factor a particular cause, though sufficient in itself, is hindered from its normal activity. Fire normally burns wood, and yet it may be prevented from doing so when water is poured on the wood. However, Aquinas does not ask whether in this last-mentioned case the causal nexus between events still obtains. In this context he does not deal with human freedom, deliberation, and decision. He rather wishes to show that even outside the area of human activity there is still some contingency, at least in the sense that events are not invariably connected with the same causes always and necessarily producing the same effects.[104] In some cases an effect, being acciden-

---

[101]*In Peri Hermeneias*, I, 14, n. 186. In his criticism Aquinas refers to Aristotle: Dicit (scil. Aristoteles) enim quod non omne quod fit habet causam, sed solum illud quod est per se. Sed illud quod est per accidens non habet causam; quia proprie non est ens, sed magis ordinatur cum non ente, ut etiam Plato dixit; *In libros Metaphysicorum*, ed. Cathala-Spiazzi (Marietti), VI, 3, nn. 1200-1201.

[102]*In Peri Hermeneias*, I, 14, n. 188. What is accidental is not linked to a particular antecedent factor that always produces the same effect.

[103]*In Peri Hermeneias*, I, 14, n. 186: Similiter etiam haec est falsa, quod posita causa etiam sufficienti, necesse est effectum poni: non enim omnis causa est talis (etiamsi sufficiens sit) quod eius effectus impediri non possit.

[104]Quite obviously what Aquinas attempts to show is that a particular cause does not always and inevitably produce the same effect, even within the physical world. Consequently, a future event is not always predictable, not only because our knowledge of things is deficient, but because reality itself is open to various possibilities. One could say that reality has more than one future. It bears within itself the possibility of various future developments, although each of them will have a causal nexus with antecedent factors.

tal, results from an accidental antecedent. In other cases the result may be prevented from being produced because of the interference of some other factor. It is in this sense that Thomas rejects the unbreakable connection between causes and effects as it was presented by the Stoics.

Aquinas does not attribute the second position on fate to any particular school. He vaguely refers to defenders of this view by noting that it is held by "some" (*quidam*).[105] In fact it is an ancient and widespread doctrine and was followed by some in the thirteenth century. According to this view, fate is the influence exercised by heavenly bodies on all that occurs on earth, not only on physical events, but even on human behavior.[106] As already indicated, Aquinas opposes this doctrine as regards human activity since intellect and will are not corporeal powers. They are joined to the body because the soul is its substantial form; but thinking and willing are not corporeal activities since they are not exercised by means of any bodily organ.[107] In this respect there is considerable difference between intellectual activity and sense perception. Sensible knowledge is always performed with the help of bodily organs. Consequently, the heavenly bodies cannot have any direct influence on an incorporeal power. They can only influence it indirectly by means of the sensitive powers. These sensitive powers, however, can never necessitate the intellect or the will, since the latter clearly transcend the lower level of knowledge and desire.[108]

Finally, fate may be understood in a third way. According to this view whatever in this world seems to result from fortune and chance is to be referred back to divine providence, to which fate itself is

---

[105]*In Peri Hermeneias*, I, 14, n. 189.

[106]*In Peri Hermeneias*, I, 14, n. 189: tentaverunt (scil. quidam) reducere omnes effectus hic inferius provenientes in aliquam causam per se, quam ponebant esse virtutem caelestium corporum in qua ponebant *fatum*, dicentes nihil aliud esse fatum quam vim positionis syderum.

[107]*In Peri Hermeneias*, I, 14, n. 189. In this respect Aquinas introduced an important distinction between two kinds of dependence. The soul may be dependent upon the body as upon an object; it may also be dependent upon it as upon a necessary instrument. In the case of intellectual knowledge the mind does not exercise its activity with the help of a corporeal organ; it depends, however, upon the body as an object (*In De Anima*, ed. A.M. Pirotta, I, 2, n. 19).

[108]*In Peri Hermeneias*, I, 14, n. 189: Manifestum autem est quod passiones virium sensitivarum non inferunt necessitatem rationi et voluntati.

subject.[109] Aquinas undoubtedly here has in mind the teaching of Boethius and Albert the Great. Thomas strongly defends the view that nothing escapes from divine providence, not even that which is thought to happen by chance. In God there is no composition or multiplicity. Thinking and willing coincide with the perfection of the divine being. Nothing can exist without participating in this fullness of being. Hence nothing can ever happen without depending on divine providence.[110] Does not this kind of dependence exclude any kind of contingency either in the physical world or in human action? Not according to Aquinas, since God, as the source and ultimate principle of all necessity and contingency, is himself beyond necessity and contingency.[111] Even though human activity is constantly dependent on divine creation, it is not determined. On the contrary, it finds its ultimate condition of possibility in the freedom of the creative act.

May fate be regarded as an effect of divine providence? In this sense, providence would be the universal plan or order as it exists in God's mind, while destiny would be the realization of this plan or order in concrete things. Aquinas replies that this interpretation may be accepted. He himself believes, however, that it is preferable to avoid this term because it is too deeply rooted in non-Christian tradition.[112]

[109]*In Peri Hermeneias*, I, 14, n. 191: Et secundum hoc aliqui posuerunt omnia quaecumque in hoc mundo aguntur, etiam quae videntur fortuita et casualia, reduci in ordinem providentiae divinae, ex qua dicebant dependere fatum; *In libros Metaphysicorum*, VI, 3, n. 1204.

[110]*In Peri Hermeneias*, I, 14, n. 191: Unde sicut esse eius sua virtute comprehendit omne illud quod quocumque modo est, in quantum scilicet est per participationem ipsius; ita etiam suum intelligere et suum intelligibile comprehendit omnem cognitionem et omne cognoscibile; et suum velle et suum volitum comprehendit omnem appetitum et omne appetibile quod est bonum.

[111]*In Peri Hermeneias*, I, 14, n. 197: Et secundum harum conditionem causarum effectus dicuntur vel necessarii vel contingentes, quamvis omnes dependeant a voluntate divina, sicut a prima causa, quae transcendit ordinem necessitatis et contingentiae.

[112]*Quodl.* XII, q. 4; *Summa contra Gentiles*, III, 93. Cf. J. Goergen, *Des hl. Albertus Magnus' Lehre von der göttlichen Vorsehung und dem Fatum, unter besonderer Rücksicht der Vorsehungs- und Schicksalslehre des Ulrich von Strasburg* (Vechta, 1932). In the *Summa de bono* of Ulrich of Strasburg the question of fate is treated in book II, treatise 5, chapter 18 (cf. F.J. Lescoe, *God as First Principle in Ulrich of Strasbourg* [New York, 1979]).

Before concluding this survey I must mention one author who lived in the fifteenth and sixteenth centuries and who devoted an extensive treatise to this topic—Pietro Pomponazzi, the author of the *De fato*. At that time the question of human freedom was being debated. Lorenzo della Valla claimed in his *De libero arbitrio* that from a philosophical standpoint human freedom cannot be reconciled with Christian belief in divine omnipotence. There was also the exchange between Erasmus and Luther on this same topic. Pomponazzi himself maintains that the Christian position is contradictory. God is regarded as the creative source of whatever exists. Moreover, divine activity cannot fail to attain its goal. Whatever exists is a tool in the hands of God, and is used and directed by him.[113] In spite of this, Christians believe that man is free and autonomous in his decisions. According to Pomponazzi, whatever occurs in the world is determined by divine providence and fate.[114] In agreement with Boethius, he defines destiny as the well-ordered disposition of providence insofar as it is realized in the world. This applies not only to irrational beings but also to human activity.[115] According to Pomponazzi, the heavenly bodies exercise a necessitating influence on human life.[116] From a philosophical standpoint, concludes Pomponazzi, only the Stoic account of fate is coherent.[117] That of Aristotle is not fully consistent because he admits that man is free and at the same time holds for an eternal recurrence of all things. This is incompatible with human freedom.[118]

Pomponazzi is well aware that the Stoic teaching on fate is in conflict with Christian belief. From the Christian standpoint we

---

[113]*Petri Pomponatii Mantuani libri quinque de fato, de libero arbitrio et de praedestinatione*, ed. R. Lemay (Lucani, 1957). Referring to a Christian, he writes: Ponit enim Deum certitudinaliter cuncta operari nihilque sine ipso movente fieri posse et omnia esse Dei instrumenta, omnia a Deo dirigi et secundum quod ab ipso diriguntur operari; et tamen dicunt velle et nolle esse nostrum.

[114]*Libri quinque de fato*, p. 192: ideo per sullogismum divisivum necessarium est confiteri omnia de fato et inevitabili ordine divinae providentiae gubernari, nihilque in nobis esse quod fato non impellatur.

[115]*Libri quinque de fato*, p. 210: Non igitur tantum ratione carentia regulantur fato, verum et actus humani; *ibid*., p. 218.

[116]*Libri quinque de fato*, pp. 212–13.

[117]*Libri quinque de fato*, p. 202: Rationabilior igitur videtur Stoicorum opinio opinione Christianorum.

[118]*Libri quinque de fato*, p. 221.

must hold that God is omnipotent and that man is free. But what is true philosophically differs from Christian belief. As a philosopher Pomponazzi wants to hold the Stoic position.[119] There is in his attitude something quite surprising. While previous authors we have studied have tried to reconcile the doctrine of fatalism with human freedom and divine providence, Pomponazzi makes no such attempt. Apparently he is willing to accept something that is philosophically contradictory on the ground of Christian revelation.

This survey again shows that Stoicism was present in medieval thought. From the above one may conclude that the essential features of Stoic teaching on fate were preserved in the Middle Ages. Fate is not a blind and irrational power. It is rather at the origin of the well-ordered disposition of all things. On the other hand, the original Stoic fatalism has been profoundly transformed and modified under the influence of every kind of criticism and objection. In this connection I have mentioned Carneades, Alexander of Aphrodisias, Plotinus, Calcidius, Proclus, and Boethius. Thanks to these transformations, fatalism became acceptable for Neoplatonists and for Christians. Hence, it was still alive at the time of the Renaissance and even thereafter down to the present day either in more radical or more mitigated form. Even in contemporary thought the coexistence of divine power and human freedom continues to be one of the most puzzling metaphysical problems.

---

[119]*Libri quinque de fato*, p. 221: Quare Stoici videntur magis convenienter respondere. Sic itaque mihi videtur esse dicendum in sequendo Stoicorum opinionem, quamquam ut in sequenti libro dicam, haec opinio sit falsa, quoniam religioni christianae quae verissima est adversatur.

INDEX OF NAMES

Abelard, Peter, 9, 10, 14, 51-53, 58
Aeschylus, 71
Aëtius, 47 n., 71 n., 78 n.
Alan of Lille, 8, 10, 37, 38, 51
Albertanus of Brescia, 12
Albert the Great, 54, 62, 69, 70, 87-91, 94
Alcher of Clairvaux, 40
Alcuin, 35
Alexander of Aphrodisias, 17, 22 n., 23 n., 73-74, 76, 80 n., 96
Alexander of Hales, 54, 62-63
Alfanus of Salerno, 76
Amand, D., 73 n., 77 n.
Ambrose, Saint, 15 n., 48
Amin, Osman, 7, 18 n.
Ammonius, 22 n.
Andronicos of Rhodos, 2 n.
Apollinarius, 36
Apuleius, 87
Arcesilaos, 2 n.
Aristotle, 2, 4, 5-6, 7, 11, 13, 14, 17, 18, 32, 41-42, 45 n., 69, 70, 73, 74 n., 80 n., 87 n., 92 n., 95
Armstrong, A.H., 35 n., 39 n.
Arnim, J. von, 17
Arnobius Junior, 34
Aspasius, 17
Auer, A., 13 n.
Augustine, Saint, 5, 15, 28-32, 34, 35, 36, 37, 38, 40, 44
Avicenna, 18, 19

Bacon, Roger, 11
Baguette, Ch., 15
Barlaam of Seminara, 12
Baron, H., 15 n.
Basil the Great, 48 n.
Bavo of Corvey, 39
Bernardus Silvestris, 38-39

Boethius, 16, 39, 42, 85-86, 87, 88, 89, 90 n., 94, 95, 96
Bonaventure, Saint, 51, 54, 63, 68, 69 n.
Burgundio of Pisa, 76

Calcidius, 16, 80-83, 85, 96
Callus, D.A., 17 n.
Cancrini, A., 67
Carneades, 47, 73, 77, 96
Cassianus, 34
Cassiodorus, 34, 35
Charles the Bald (king of France), 35
Chenu, M.-D., 18
Chroust, A.H., 61 n.
Chrysippus, 45 n., 50, 67, 72, 73 n., 77
Chrysostom, John, 48 n.
Cicero, 9, 14-16, 27, 46-47, 48, 49, 50, 53 n., 54, 55 n., 67 n., 73 n., 74
Claudianus Mamertus, 34
Cleanthes, 3 n., 45 n., 72
Clement of Alexandria, 5, 48
Costa ben Luca, 18, 40
Courcelle, P., 15 n., 16
Crowe, M.B., 54 n., 62 n., 65 n., 66 n., 68 n., 69 n.

David of Dinant, 39
Dechanet, J.M., 10 n.
Delhaye, Ph., 9, 13 n., 35 n., 37 n., 38 n., 49 n.
Deman, Th., 48 n.
Den Boeft, J., 16
De Rijk, L.M., 12 n.
Dickly, M., 15 n.
Diogenes Laërtios, 4 n., 45 n., 55 n., 68 n., 72 n.
Dondaine, A., 12 n.
Dörrie, H., 32 n.
Dühring, I., 2 n.

97

INDEX OF NAMES

Duns Scotus, John, 65, 87, 90 n.

Eckhart, Meister, 13
Epictetus, 7, 18, 72
Epicurus, 2, 21, 47
Erasmus, 95
Eriugena, John Scotus, 87 n.
Evagrius Ponticus, 48

Faider, P., 8 n.
Faustus of Riez, 33–34
Festugière, A.J., 2 n.
Firmitius (Julius Firmicius Maternus), 88
Fortin, E.L., 34

Gagner, A., 14 n.
Gaius, 56–57, 58 n.
Galen, 18
Gauthier, R.-A., 48, 50, 51 n.
Gawlick, G., 15 n.
Gennadius of Marseille, 34
Gerard of Cremona, 88
Gilson, E., 39
Giraldus Cambrensis, 12
Glorieux, P., 13 n.
Godfrey of St. Victor, 8
Goergen, J., 94 n.
Gomez Nogales, S., 18 n.
Grabmann, M., 87 n.
Gregory, T., 38 n., 39 n.
Gregory of Nazianzus, 48 n.
Gregory of Nyssa, 5, 48 n., 76
Grosseteste, Robert, 16
Guerric of St. Quentin, 61
Gundissalinus, 18

Haes, J., 14
Hagendahl, H., 15
Hain, L., 7 n.
Hamesse, J., 14 n.
Hebing, J., 54 n.
Henry, Prince of Anjou-Plantagenet (King Henry II of England), 9, 48
Heraclitus, 71
Hermias, 29 n.
Hierocles, 41

Hilary of Poitiers, 34
Hrabanus Maurus, 35
Hugh of St. Victor, 13, 58

Iamblichus, 41
Isaac Israeli, 19
Isidore of Seville, 56, 57, 58 n.

Jadaane, F., 18 n.
Jagu, A., 45 n.
Jerome, Saint, 5, 8 n., 36, 53
Joannes Teutonicus, 59
John Damascene, 79
John of Dambach, 13
John of La Rochelle, 62
John of Salisbury, 8, 9–10
John of Spain, 18
Justinian, 57

Lactantius, 5, 15 n., 25–27, 33, 44
Lescoe, F.J., 94 n.
Lieser, L., 11 n.
Longpré, E., 11 n.
Lotharius I (king of Germany), 35
Lottin, O., 54 n., 57 n., 58 n., 59 n., 60, 61 n., 62 n., 63 n., 64 n.
Lucilius, 8
Luther, 95

Macarius of Egypt, 27
Macarius Scotus, 37
McDonnell, K., 66 n.
Marcus Aurelius, 41
Martin of Bracara, 14
Milton-Valente, P., 15 n.
Moncho Pascual, J.R., 55 n.

Nemesius of Emesa, 5, 32–33, 34, 76–80
Nicholas Trivet, 12
Norpoth, L., 40 n.
Nothdurft, Klaus-Dieter, 8 n., 14 n.

Odo of Cambrai, 36, 37
Oresme, Nicholas, 13
Origen, 5, 34 n., 36, 48 n., 81
Otho of Freising, 11

Index of Names

Panaetius, 5, 15, 50, 54, 67, 68
Paul, Saint, 8
Paulus Alvarus of Cordoba, 36
Pelzer, A., 17 n.
Pembroke, S.G., 55 n.
Pernoud, Régine, 1 n.
Perraut, William, 11, 12 n.
Peter Cantor, 10, 51
Peter Lombard, 52, 53–54
Peter of Spain, 12
Peter of Tarentaise, 64
Petrarch, 12
Philip of Harvengt, 8
Philip the Chancellor, 54, 61, 68, 69 n.
Philopator, 77
Philopon, Jean, 40 n.
Pichon, R., 26 n.
Pierce, C.A., 67
Pirotti, Niccolo, 7
Plato, 2 n., 16, 29, 32, 39 n., 42 n., 81, 88 n., 89 n., 92 n.
Plotinus, 4, 15, 27, 28, 29, 32, 37, 40, 75–76, 79, 96
Plutarch, 67 n.
Pohlenz, M., 57 n., 67, 77 n.
Politian, Angelus, 7
Pomponazzi, Pietro, 42 n., 95–96
Porphyry, 27, 32 n., 41
Portalié, E., 31 n.
Posidonius, 5, 67, 68, 72
Potts, T.C., 68 n.
Proclus, 41, 68 n., 83–85, 86, 96
Pseudo-Plutarch, 18, 75 n.
Ptolemy, 88, 90
Pythagoras, 3

Quintilian, 8, 9

Rand, E.K., 15
Ratramnus of Corbie, 35, 37–38
Reale, G., 2 n., 3 n.
Reynolds, L.D., 8 n., 14 n.
Roland of Cremona, 61
Rommen, H., 66 n.
Rouse, R.H., 13 n.

Sassen, F., 16

Schmidt, Th., 48 n.
Seneca, 4, 8–14, 22 n., 23 n., 27, 29 n., 39, 46, 47 n., 48, 49, 50, 67, 72, 88
Seneca (the rhetor), 8, 13
Sextius, A., 67 n.
Sextus Empiricus, 17, 22 n., 23 n.
Seyr, F., 23 n.
Simon of Bosiniano, 59
Simplicius, 7, 17
Socrates, 2 n., 39 n., 69 n.
Spanneut, M., 1 n., 5 n., 34 n., 35, 45 n., 48 n.
Stephen Tempier (bishop of Paris), 41–42
Stobaeus, 67 n., 72 n.

Tatian, 24
Tertullian, 5, 23–25, 26, 29 n., 33, 36, 44
Testard, M., 15
Thales, 21
Theodoretus, 71 n.
Theodorus, 83
Thierry of Chartres, 38
Thomas Aquinas, Saint, 11, 12, 15–16, 17, 18, 19 n., 39–41, 42–44, 54, 55, 58, 63–64, 65, 69–70, 77, 87 n., 91–94
Thomas Hibernicus, 13
Thomas of York, 11
Thorndike, L., 87 n.
Tropia, L., 17 n.

Ulpian, 57, 62
Ulrich of Strasburg, 87, 94 n.

Valla, Lorenzo della, 95
Van Steenkiste, C., 16
Verbeke, G., 2 n., 4 n., 5 n., 17 n., 25 n., 40 n., 41 n., 42 n., 43 n., 46 n., 68 n., 80 n.
Victorinus, 29
Vincentius Victor, 34
Vincent of Beauvais, 11
Virgil, 39
Von Ivanka, E., 15 n.

Walther of St. Victor, 13

William of Auvergne, 51
William of Auxerre, 60, 62, 63
William of Conches, 9, 38–39, 48–50
William of Malmesbury, 10
William of Moerbeke, 17, 73, 83
William of Ockham, 65–66

William of St. Thierry, 10, 36–37
William of Sherwood, 12
Wolfson, H.A., 18 n.

Zeno of Citium, 2, 4 n., 39, 45 n., 71–72

INDEX OF TOPICS

Anticipations, natural (προλήψεις), 47, 55
Aristotelianism, 2, 5-7, 17, 19

Conscience (*syneidesis*), 49, 54, 62, 67-70

Epicureanism, 2, 21, 32
Evolution of the world (history), 3, 22, 30, 31, 43, 45, 52, 60, 72, 78, 79, 80, 87-88, 91

Fate, 3, 16, 30, 52, 71-96
Foreknowledge, divine, 82, 84-85, 86
Freedom, human, 3, 31, 37, 44; and necessity, 17, 42-44, 71-96

Gnosticism, 24-25, 27, 28 n.
God as corporeal in Christian thought, 24-27, 28-29, 34

Impassibility (*apatheia*), 24, 25, 48

Law of nations (*ius gentium*), 57-58
Lekton, 22 n., 23

Magnanimity, 48, 50-51
Materialism, 4, 10, 21-44

Natural law, 46-47, 52-53, 54, 56-67, 68, 69, 70
Neoplatonism, 4-5, 28, 32, 34, 35 n., 40, 41, 44, 81, 87, 89, 96

Oikeiosis, 47, 55, 59, 62, 64
Orthodoxy, Christian, and Stoicism, 5, 6 n.

Pantheism, 4, 10, 33, 58. *See also* World-soul
φαντασία, 18
Pneuma, 23, 24, 27, 41
Practical syllogism, Aristotelian doctrine of, 62, 69-70
Providence, divine, 5, 26, 32, 71, 72, 76, 78-80, 81, 83-84, 85-86, 87, 88-89, 90 n., 93-94, 95, 96
Pythagoreanism, 2-3, 36, 67 n.

Reason, Divine. *See* World-soul

Seminal reasons, 4-5, 30-32, 91
Skepticism, 2, 28
Soul(s), human: materialistic conception of, 18-19, 23-27, 33-34, 35, 36-37, 41; origin and nature of, 18-19, 23-27, 29, 32-37, 38, 39-44; unity vs. multiplicity of, 35, 37-39
Spirit, immanent divine. *See* World-soul
Spirit (*spiritus*), 18-19, 23, 26-27, 35, 37, 40 n.
συγκατάθεσις, 18, 51
Synderesis, 53-56, 59, 61-62, 63, 64, 67, 68, 69, 70

Traducianism, 25, 36, 38, 44

World-soul (Divine Reason, immanent divine Spirit), 3, 4, 22, 23, 26, 28-29, 37, 38-39, 41, 43, 44, 45, 47, 49, 52, 56, 58, 71, 74 n., 78, 81

LIBRARY OF DAVIDSON COLLEGE

Books on regular loan may be checked out for **two weeks**. Books must be presented at the Circulation Desk in order to be renewed.

A fine is charged after date due.